Opening the Marketplace
to Small Enterprise

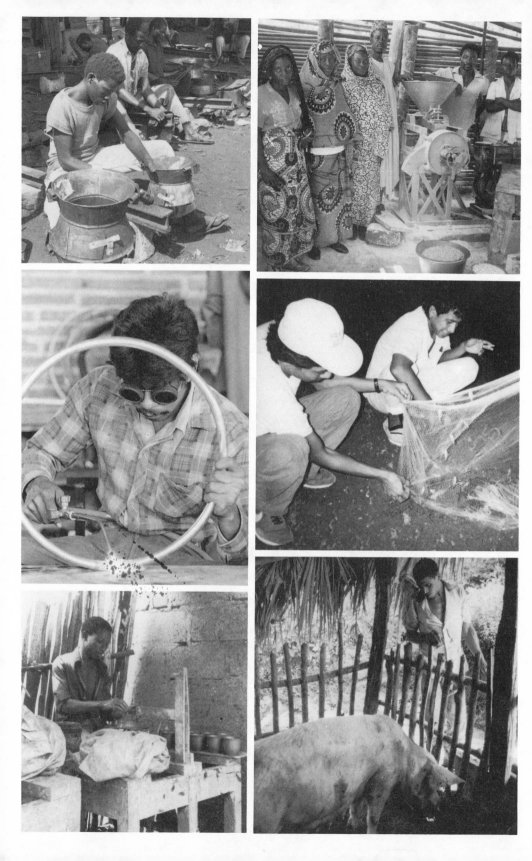

Opening the Marketplace to Small Enterprise

✦ ✦ ✦

Where Magic Ends and Development Begins

Ton de Wilde
Stijntje Schreurs
with
Arleen Richman

KUMARIAN PRESS

Opening the Marketplace to Small Enterprise: Where Magic Ends and Development Begins

Published in the United States of America by Kumarian Press, Inc.
630 Oakwood Avenue, Suite 119, West Hartford, Connecticut 06110-1529 USA
ISBN 0-931816-88-2 (U.S.) cloth   ISBN 0-931816-87-4 (U.S.) paper

Published in the United Kingdom by Intermediate Technology Publications Ltd.
103-105 Southampton Row, London WC1B 4HH, United Kingdom
ISBN 1-85339-093-3 (U.K.)

Printed in the United States of America

Cover design by Laura Augustine   Edited by Barbara A. Conover
Typeset by Rosanne Pignone   Proofread by Beth Penney
Index prepared by Alan M. Greenberg

Printed on acid-free paper by McNaughton and Gunn, Inc.

Library of Congress Cataloging-in-Publication Data

Wilde, Ton de.
    Opening the marketplace to small enterprise : where magic ends and development begins / Ton de Wilde, Stijntje Schreurs.
       p.   cm. — (Kumarian Press library of management for development)
    Includes bibliographical references and index.
    ISBN 0-931816-88-2 (cloth : alk. paper). — ISBN 0-931816-87-4 (pbk. : alk. paper)
    1. Small business—Developing countries—Case studies. 2. Small business—Government policy—Developing countries—Case studies.
I. Schreurs, Stijntje, 1964–   . II. Title. III. Series.
HD2346.D43W55   1991
338.6'42'091724—dc20
                                           91-7371

95   94   93   92   91   5   4   3   2   1

✦ Contents

✦ Tables

✦ Abbreviations

AATP	Arusha Appropriate Technology Project
ACB	Anglo-Colombiana Bank
ACM	Asociación de Cafeculturos de Moquita
ADEPE	Asociación para el Desarrollo de la Provincia Espaillat (Association for Development in Espaillat Province, Dominican Republic)
APICA	Association pour le Promotion des Initiatives Communitaries Africaines (Association for the Promotion of Community Initiatives in Africa)
APORCI	Asociación Porcicultores de Cibao
APORLI	Asociación Porcicultores de Licey
ATI	Appropriate Technology International (United States)
BARD	Banco Agricola de la República Dominicana
BIAO	Banque Internationale d'Afrique Occidentale (Bank in Cameroon)
BICIC	Banque Internationale pour le Commerce et l'Industrie du Cameroun (Bank in Cameroon)
BIPIK	Small Industry Support Program (Indonesia)
BOI	Board of Investment
CAFESA	Campesinos Federados de Salcedo (Federation of farmers in Dominican Republic)
CAMARTEC	Centre for Agricultural Mechanization and Rural Technology (Tanzania)
CATMI	Cameroon Agricultural Tools Manufacturing Industry
CEF	Convertible Equity Fund
CENIP	National Center for Animal Investigation (Dominican Republic)
CFP	Corporación Financieria Popular
CIMPA	Centro de Investigación y Mejoramiento de Producción Animal (Center of Investigation and Improvement of Animal Production, Dominican Republic)
COONA-PROCE	Cooperación Naciónal de Productores de Cerdos (Dominican Republic)

CRDB	Cooperative and Rural Development Bank
CRRV	Corporación Regionál del Rehabilitación del Valle del Cauca (Regional Rehabilitation Corporation, Cauca Valley)
CUSA	Credit Union and Savings Association (Zambia)
DAS	Development Association of Santiago
FAO	Food and Agriculture Organization
FC	Carvajal Foundation (development organization in Colombia)
FES	Foundation for Advanced Education
FESA	Federación Equipos Sociales y Agrarios
FONADER	National Fund for Rural Development (Cameroon)
GDP	gross domestic product
GNP	gross national product
GRAMA	ADEPE's feed processing center
IAC	industrially advanced countries
IADB	Inter American Development Bank
IBRD	International Bank for Reconstruction and Development (World Bank)
IFAD	International Fund for Agricultural Development
IFC	International Finance Corporation
ILO	International Labor Organization
IMF	International Monetary Fund
ITDG	Intermediate Technology Development Group (United Kingdom)
JICA	Japan International Cooperation Agency
KENGO	Kenya Energy Nongovernmental Organizations Association
KFW	German development bank
KIDC	Kilimanjaro Industrial Development Center
KIE	Kenya Industrial Estates
KREDP	Kenya Renewable Energy Development Project
MFA	Moca Farmer's Association
MIDENO	North West Province Development Authority (Cameroon)
MOE	Kenya Ministry of Energy and Regional Development
NBC	National Bank of Commerce
NGO	nongovernmental organization
OECD	Organization for Economic Cooperation and Development
ORD	Organización de Revolucionarios Desabilitados
OSU	Outgrowers Service Unit
PAFSAT	Promotion of Adapted Farming Systems Based on Animal Traction
PDA	Planning and Development Association (Thailand)
PQLI	Physical Quality of Life Index
RSIE	rural small industrial enterprise
SCB	Societe Camerounaise de Banque (bank in Cameroon)
SIDO	Small Industry Development Organization (Tanzania)
SMIDA	small industrial development agency

TAMTU	Tanzanian Agricultural Machinery Project
TCA	Tanzanian Ceramic Association
UNICEF	United Nations International Children's Fund
UNIDO	United National Industrial Development Organization
UNIFEM	United Nations Development Fund for Women
USAID	United States Agency for International Development
USDA	United States Department of Agriculture
VCC	Venture capital company
YDD	Yayasan Dian Desa (development organization in Indonesia)

✦ Acknowledgments

THERE WOULD BE no book if it were not for the work of the people who actually participated in the projects and the work of the implementing organizations. Although these organizations and their work are discussed in detail in the actual case studies, the authors acknowledge the cooperation of the following Appropriate Technology International (ATI) project partners:

Maize Mills, Cameroon; Association for the Promotion of African Initiatives (APICA); and B. A. Anguh Agricultural Tools Manufacturing and the North West Province Development Authority (MIDENO). Mr. Alexander Lantum, Credit Advisor to the National Fund for Rural Development (FONADER), is to be singled out for his insights and his help in coordinating visits to the women's groups and the banks.

Improved *Jikos*, Kenya: Kenya Energy Nongovernmental Organizations Association (KENGO).

Rural Potteries, Tanzania: Centre for Agricultural Mechanization and Rural Technology (CAMARTEC), especially Frank Wiso, and the helpful insights of Aliasghar Sherif of Sherif Dewji & Sons, Ltd.

Shrimp Cultivation, Indonesia: Yayasan Dian Desa (YDD), especially Anton Soedjarwo and Didik Wiryadi.

Swine Feed, Dominican Republic: Pedro Ascona and the staff of Centro de Investigación y Mejoramiento de Producción Animal (CIMPA).

Wheelchairs, Colombia: Fundación Carvajal (FC), notably Senora Maria Rosario Carvajal.

The authors are grateful for the help given by several ATI staff members whose firsthand knowledge of project activities helped us understand what had taken place and guided us in formulating their conclusions. Special thanks to Project Officer Edward Perry (maize mill), Project Officer Richard Bowman (swine feed), Program Director Valeria Budinich and consultant Ralf Hotchkiss (wheelchairs), Program Economist Eric L. Hyman (*jikos*) and Program Evaluator John Skibiak (swine feed), who took time to review several drafts of the pertinent case studies, despite their otherwise hectic schedules.

The authors also wish to thank Lucy Creevey and George McRobie, whose helpful comments on early drafts were exceptionally valuable in finalizing the book; G. William Watson and Janet Trucker, who prepared the final manuscript and suffered through endless changes and revisions; copy readers Susan Klein, Jennifer Lavan and Pamela Magasich; and Scott Ripley, who helped with the word processing.

Last but not least, a word of thanks for Kumarian Press publisher Krishna Sondhi and editor Jenna Dixon, who have been instrumental in shaping this book's final form.

✦ Introduction: "The Magic of the Marketplace"

WHEN GOVERNOR REAGAN became President Reagan, the magic of the marketplace became the buzzword for a strategy replacing the basic, human needs approach to development characteristic of the late 1970s. "The magic of the marketplace" was expected to rescue a growing number of developing countries from bankruptcy. The budget deficits of these countries reflected, in part, the enormous amounts of money they spent to service foreign debt. This debt was incurred to finance investments in huge industrialization efforts, to pay for skyrocketing energy costs and to fund programs to alleviate poverty, decrease malnutrition and increase school enrollment—long-term investments in national human resources.

With limited resources, budgets had to be trimmed and expenditures decreased. The proposed solution was to cut all expenditures that did not contribute to economic growth. A popular edict was "Let the forces of the marketplace determine the direction of the economy." Governments should continue only those services for which there is a demand—a demand demonstrated by the willingness and ability of people to pay for those services. In short, allow the "magic of the marketplace" to function.

A few years later it became clear that, although the magic worked for some countries (many countries did show a renewed positive annual growth), the panacea proved to be a myth for populations not yet in the marketplace. The Physical Quality of Life Index (PQLI) for many countries decreased dramatically. Infant mortality and malnutrition increased while school enrollments decreased. The gap between the rich and the poor widened. To balance their budgets, governments needed to decide what services should be eliminated and in what type of production to invest. Governments—affluent and poor,

1

donor and recipient—needed to re-examine the concept of development.

What is Development?

If, according to market definitions, a service or product is not in demand, is it still needed for development? For example, if people in a particular rural area do not have the money to pay for safe drinking water, does this mean that, for them, safe drinking water is not a development priority?

In most countries, we find a situation analogous to that of the global economy: Some countries have a substantial share of the international market and others do not. Table A-1 provides statistics about these differences. This table, however, as is the case with most statistics, does not really tell us what it means to use the equivalent of 86 kg of fuel oil per year, which is the average amount of energy used by a person in the poorest thirty-seven countries, compared with 4,952 kg of oil, which is the average consumed by a person in the nineteen richest countries. Nor does it indicate any of the additional factors that accompany a high consumption level, such as production of acid rain and the destruction of the ozone layer.

Table A-1   Some Development Indicators for Two Groups of Countries, 1986

Indicator	37 Poorest Countries	19 Industrially Advanced Countries
Population (millions)	658	742
GNP/capita (US$)	200	12,960
Foreign trade (deficit)/ surplus (US$b)[a]	(11.8)	67
Savings as percentage of GDP	7	21
Life expectancy at birth (yr)	52	76
Population living in rural areas (%)	80	25
Population working in agriculture (%)[b]	71	7
Fertilizer use (hundred gm/ha)	234	1,164
Index of food production (1979–1981)	101	103
Energy consumption per capita (kg oil equivalent)	86	4,952
Population growth, 1980–1986	2.8	0.6
Population per doctor	17,670	550
Population per nurse	7,130	180
Daily calorie intake	2,100	3,357

Source: World Development Report 1988 (New York: Oxford University Press, 1988).
[a] Merchandise trade only, i.e., excluding services.
[b] Data for 1980.

The people who use the marketplace—the people who operate in the formal economy—are concerned with the value of capital. For them, a stock market crash or an increased trade deficit can create havoc. For the poor—the people who cannot enter the marketplace—a plummeting stock market is of no interest; they have no capital or stock market investments to be concerned about. They struggle just to grow enough food. Rain or sunshine is more important to them than statistics or the budget. Yet, they are an integral part of our world economy.

In the mid-1970s, at the height of the oil distribution crisis, and following the various reports of the Club of Rome,[1] we were warned that our natural resources were running out. Oil would no longer be available; some primary raw materials such as copper would be obtainable only through recycling. We were and are consuming potential resources that should be the inheritance not only of our children and their children, but also of the children of our neighbors, people in the Third World who are entering the era of economic development. The poor in the informal sectors and the rural poor are now trying to obtain the material wealth and luxuries they see every day on television—on sets such as the one located in front of the hut of a village chief in Mali, which is watched by the entire village. They are entering an era when they, too, expect to buy their own television sets and motorcycles and live in the comfort of air-conditioned rooms. Unfortunately, this is what we—the mass media, the politicians, the economists and the development practitioners—have led them to believe. Yet this dream will come true for only a very small percentage of the people living in the Third World.

The industrially advanced countries (IACs) not only are consuming resources that cannot be replaced, but they are destroying the environment, which cannot be replenished. Not everybody will agree with this statement. Many economists, scientists and technologists argue that it is an overly pessimistic world view. They say that we have to believe in technology. Technology will solve these problems; it will create new forms of energy and will heal the ozone layer, just as it has turned once-useless material, for example, rock phosphate, into productive resources. They would argue that our lack of answers should motivate us to support technology development and lobby for larger allocations, for more funds for research and development in our national budgets.[2] The evidence to date, however, does not warrant such optimism.

The Politics of Development: Unemployment and Work Ethos

So far, we have discussed only the physical aspects of development—and the associated problems of consumption of resources that cannot be replaced. Development also includes the creation of jobs. Our inability to create jobs, to create the conditions under which people can earn a living, is rapidly leading to the next major world crisis—the unemployment crisis. Statistics indicate that between 1990 and 2000 another 1.2 billion people will enter the labor force. These are not the unborn. These people are already alive. About a quarter of them will find some form of employment in agriculture, industry or services. The remaining 900 million people will be unable to find a regular source of income. Yet, the majority of these people will want to start a family, and they expect to have some of the material joys of life. They will have been told and they will believe that a job and a family are the important elements of life. Many of them are already disillusioned and many more will join their ranks when it becomes clear that, despite promises by politicians, governments and visiting dignitaries, there is no job and no income. Is it surprising that the most aggressive will want to take by force what society does not offer them? The belief that ideals must inspire revolutionary or guerrilla movements has already been eroded; more and more revolutions have become struggles between the haves and have nots.

We must deal with these issues. We must stimulate a more equal distribution of income and resources, take steps to protect the environment and create employment that will allow the millions of unemployed to earn a regular income. To do that, however, the traditional paradigm of economic growth has to change. Development priorities will need to be redefined. Is the production of consumer goods in capital-intensive, large-scale industries the most cost-effective use of scarce development resources?

But is it realistic to expect policymakers to enact legislation contrary to the promises that brought many of them into office? Are the policymakers not expected to uphold the dream that everybody can be wealthy, that all citizens can have a car, electricity and tap water in their homes? Are the policymakers going to admit that material wealth is not possible for all?

If policymakers find it necessary to promote this dream, that would explain why so many Third World governments follow the policies of the IACs. Like their counterparts in the IACs, they promised their citizens instant development, often despite their knowledge of its pitfalls. Unfortunately, even if Third World governments wanted to follow different policies, economic realities would intrude.

The many conflicting interests—to stimulate rapid economic growth, to preserve scarce resources, to protect the environment, to create employment opportunities for all in society and to service debt incurred by former politicians (used to stimulate a rapid economic growth that did not take place)—make policymaking extremely difficult.

Allowing Market Forces to Operate: The Magic of the Marketplace

One solution to the development problem, the neo-liberal approach[3] currently being followed by major bi- and multilateral development organizations and governments, is to reduce government interference (and also government assistance). This policy would allow the magic of the marketplace to solve the problems of development. It is argued, after all, that this is what made the United States economically strong.

The neo-liberal model can be summarized as follows: First, economic growth is more important than other development considerations; neo-liberals argue that it is better to have more unequal shares of a large cake than equal shares of a small cake. Second, high rates of economic growth are expected to lead to a trickle down of benefits to the population at large (despite thirty years of experience to the contrary). Third, neo-liberals do believe in the magic of the marketplace. Growth is said to be maximized in the context of perfectly functioning markets both for physical inputs and for services. Fourth, they claim that state intervention is characterized by rent-seeking behavior. This occurs when state employees use their control over quotas, concessions and other policies to extract a nonproductive rent from producers and consumers. Finally, no matter how imperfect markets tend to be, the neo-liberals believe that markets are more likely to succeed than is state intervention. Thus, the response to market failure should be not a larger role for the state, but a drive to reduce market imperfections.

As will be explained later in detail, withdrawal of state intervention to bolster the well-being of the large majority of the poor has immediate, drastically negative effects, especially on welfare and health indicators. Some of the advocates of the neo-liberal approach would argue, in private discussions, that one needs to accept these dramatic increases in malnutrition and/or infant mortality. They would say that those societies probably do not have the resources to sustain so many people.

The irony of this situation is twofold. First, there is a strong debate whether the magic of the marketplace has driven the economy of the United States.[4] The medicine offered to other countries did not provide the hoped-for cure in the United States itself. During the time when the magic of the marketplace philosophy was being heralded, the United States' budget deficit increased from US$127.9 billion in 1982 to US$173.2 billion in 1987. Its international trade balance plummeted from a US$26.3 billion credit in 1982 to a US$94.7 billion deficit as of 1988.[5] Income distribution in the United States widened, and the number of people below the poverty line increased both in absolute and relative terms.

Second, about three-quarters of the world's population would not be able to benefit from this magic. These people—billions of them—do not have the surplus production that would bring them to any marketplace, either to sell their produce or to buy the produce of others.

The People Who Cannot Enter the Marketplace

Notwithstanding the debate among academics and party ideologues, the international economic environment dictates actions along the lines of the magic of the marketplace philosophy described above. Many Third World governments realized that they cannot service the debts they incurred in the 1970s.[6] Yet, under the terms of existing agreements, these loans need to be repaid with interest. Thus, Third World governments, by necessity or inspired by the new development philosophy, cut their budgets. Bowing to pressure from International Monetary Fund/World Bank (IMF/WB) sources, structural changes were made to bring the countries' economies back on an economic growth path—a prerequisite for additional IMF/WB financing.

The implementation of these policies had a dramatic effect on the people who could not enter the marketplace, the people living below the poverty line. For a full description of the causes and effects of these policies we refer to *Adjustment with a Human Face,* by Cornia, Jolly and Stewart.[7]

Consider some examples from this book regarding the impacts of these relatively indiscriminate cuts in government expenditure. In Brazil, the cuts in government spending that delayed the implementation of the Expanded Program of Immunization in Sao Paulo State led to an outbreak of deadly communicable diseases among children. A study of Ghana illustrates the sharp increases in incidence of infectious diseases—and specific mortality rates—following cuts in primary health care expenditure.[8] Reduction in food subsidies in Sri Lanka led to an increase in third-degree malnutrition among the children of the poorest sector of the population. Similarly, the cancellation of a government-financed child-feeding program in 1983 in Chile led to a statistically significant nationwide increase in child mortality, which began to decline as soon as the program was reintroduced.[9] On a more general note, a UNICEF study team found that the nutritional status of children deteriorated in all but two of the ten countries for which detailed data were available. Education has also been affected. Seven out of ten countries experienced declines in primary enrollment and completion rates or serious deterioration in the quality of education.

In their conclusion, Cornia and his coauthors observe, among other factors, that while improvements in the current account balance were recorded in 56 percent of IMF-assisted countries, in the 1980s growth deteriorated or did not improve in the first program year in almost 60 percent of these countries. Between 1980 and 1983, real investment levels also declined or stagnated in almost 60 percent of countries with IMF-assisted programs. With falling output and, at best, mixed evidence about changes in income distribution in many developing countries, the number of impoverished people in adjusting countries increased.

It is not possible methodologically to attribute precise causal responsibility for this deterioration in human conditions. In many cases, the pernicious effects of world recession, declining capital flows and high interest rates, as well as local weather conditions, have represented a major obstacle to the functioning of such policies. The evidence of the 1980s however, points to the inability of the current approach to adjustment to sustain short- and medium-term growth while bringing about improvements of the external balance in the prevailing international environment. The observed drop in investment levels appears particularly alarming as it tends to compromise current and future growth.[10]

As will be discussed in detail in Chapter 1, government intervention in rural income-generating activities has not brought about the desired results. Intentionally or not, government intervention in the small-scale industrial sector has denied thousands of people the opportunity to earn an income.

Does Development Mean
That the Poor Support the Rich?

Can we, in all honesty, continue to support what still is called development? Do the IACs need to extract more than US$40 billion annually from poor Third World countries in debt service and other payments? Do the modern industrial nations need to continue to consume so much that they jeopardize their children's future and destroy forests, pollute water and taint food? Is this the meaning of development?

"How long can we maintain the belief that economic growth is equal to development and is the foundation for democracy?"[11] How long can politicians maintain the myth that we all can live like the glamorous film stars projected on television screens, including those people who live in villages where more than half of the population is undernourished and who lack an income to afford even the basic necessities promised by their politicians? How much longer can Third World governments pay interest on foreign debt to sustain the lifestyle of the people living in the developed countries and then feed, clothe and give work to the people in their own countries?

What Is Next?

Where is the cutoff? When do we stop satisfying our desire for material well-being at the expense of the environment? When do we stop placing the burden for sustaining our lifestyle on the shoulders of our children or the children of the poor in the Third World? Where or when does a state stop gathering material wealth?

We need a new ethos, a value system that balances the material and social aspects of life. In such a value system, poverty alleviation programs would be combined with income-generation programs. Success would be measured not only by material achievements that cannot be sustained by the available world resources, but also by our ability to share wealth—both in terms of worldly goods and in terms of spiritual resources. Ideally, this new ethos would be translated into new economic and social objectives. More equal income distribution would be given a priority higher than that of increases in GNP. People living in rural areas would have the same opportunities as those in urban areas to be employed, to earn an adequate income and to take risks to establish their own enterprises.

But a new ethos is still only a dream, and the rural poor in the Third World cannot live on dreams. They need concrete actions to take the initial steps to help themselves. This book describes six such actions—projects in which local organizations have intervened to enable their members or associates to produce surplus goods and get their products into the marketplace, not through magic but through an innovative approach mostly developed by the people themselves and a good portion of hard work.

In Chapter 1, the context of the six cases is described. The magic of the marketplace was a response to the ineffectiveness of supply interventions in the late 1970s. Thus, although magic does not work, neither in general did supply-side intervention. Chapter 1 reviews some of the general characteristics of these supply-side interventions and why they failed. It also reviews in depth the economic and political environment in which small-scale operations have to work. Chapters 2 through 7 describe six cases, each of which used a different mechanism to allow people to enter the marketplace. The theme that unites all the chapters is the assumption that people who do not now have a place in the market can—through the provision of innovative technical, institutional and financial assistance—enter the marketplace in a sustainable manner. The case studies share the experience of attempts, both successful and not so successful, to start self-sustainable rural production systems that create new markets by creating demand pull. Each case study looks at an enterprise as an open system and analyzes where it gets its raw material and sells its output, what technology is involved and how it was improved to gain market access for the products produced with the help of that technology.

To provide a theoretical framework in which the various approaches can be classified, the case studies described here are divided into three broad categories: financing potential buyers, enhancing the quality of the products of small enterprises and providing small-scale producers with access to markets and inputs they would not have if only market forces prevailed.

Buyer Financing

In many rural areas of developing countries, although demand exists for a particular product, the potential purchasers cannot buy the product. The cost of the product—for example, a maize mill or a palm oil press—is beyond their means, even though such a product will ultimately generate income, and the potential buyers do not have access to credit. One approach used to correct this problem is buyer financing, making arrangements to assist buyers to obtain credit or to put in place financial instruments that enable them to purchase the products of the enterprises. The maize milling project in Cameroon (Chapter 2) and the wheelchair production in Colombia (Chapter 3) are examples of this type of financial intervention.

To enable women's and other local groups in the North West Province of Cameroon to purchase the maize mill, a lease/purchase scheme was instituted. Provisions incorporated in the lease/purchase agreement can stimulate local maintenance and repair of the product, which are especially important when a new technology is being introduced. In most lease/purchase agreements, the owner (the producing enterprise or the credit agency) is responsible for any extraordinary maintenance and repair associated with the product, thus reducing the risk undertaken by the buyer. To reduce risks even further, the contract could suspend the buyer's payments for any period when the product is not working. On the other hand, to stimulate local maintenance and repair, the lease/purchase agreement can stipulate that if the user takes the responsibility for maintenance and repair, he or she earns a rebate. Finally, a lease/purchase agreement may offer the buyer the choice of paying in cash or in kind. Obviously this would be done only for a product that is easily marketable and one for which prices do not fluctuate significantly.

The wheelchair project in Colombia used a traditional loan (consumer credit) scheme. When this project was conceptualized, it was envisioned that the rehabilitation organization not only would administer the loan but also would work with the business community to secure jobs for the prospective wheelchair rider. An employed wheelchair rider should be able to pay off the loan from earnings and would be less financially dependent on family, friends or charitable institutions. Translating this ideal into reality, however, proved far more difficult than was anticipated. In a market where labor is abundant, businesses appear to prefer to donate part of the cost of the wheelchair rather than to employ a wheelchair rider.

The contract to implement the village pottery project in Tanzania (Chapter 4) stipulated that loan funds were to be made available for village potters—the buyers—to purchase fire bricks and glazing material from another enterprise, a ceramic industry that received financial and technical assistance from a foreign nongovernmental organization (NGO) to begin producing these products. Because of the lack of institutional capacity of the implementing agency, by the end of 1989 no financing had been made available to the village potters.

Enhancing the Quality of Products of Small-Scale Enterprises

Consumption/demand can also be stimulated by increasing public confidence in a product. This is the aim of most advertising both in industrialized countries and in the formal sector in developing countries. However, in economies where consumers have little surplus cash, people first need to be assured of the quality of the products they buy. In promoting the use of improved *jikos* in Kenya (Chapter 5), ceramic liner production had to be mechanized in order to reduce the cracking rate. Developing a jigger jolly, part of the molding equipment used in making *jikos,* and instituting other production improvements reduced the cracking rate of ceramic liners from more than 30 percent to slightly more than 2 percent. The urban middle class dwellers realized that the improved *jiko* was a quality product and that savings in charcoal costs in one to three months would more than offset the initial cost of the improved *jiko*, and they were eager to buy the product.

Access to Markets and Other Inputs

Swine producers in the Dominican Republic (Chapter 6) and small-scale *tambak* farmers in Indonesia (Chapter 7) were provided access to inputs previously unavailable. Financing village sales outlets for swine feed permitted farmers to buy small rations of feed. Some outlets sold the feed on credit and payment was deferred until the pigs reached market size.

In Indonesia, the *tambak* owners participating in the project were advanced feed and shrimp fry; the cost of these inputs was deducted from the proceeds of the harvested shrimp. Both the Dominican and Indonesian farmers/entrepreneurs also received assistance in marketing and transporting their produce to market. Through the associations, swine farmers learned about market conditions and currency fluctuations and received prognoses of market prices. In Indonesia, because it represented many shrimp growers, the venture capital company used its greater bargaining power to secure better prices and additional markets.

The six case studies demonstrate a nontraditional approach to stimulate the economic process. The projects described are creating markets through what might be called structured markets. Interventions are based on financing both production and consumption, not just supply and demand. Although not all projects have been successful, and some are still too new for their impact to be measured, the approach of creating markets as an integral part of the assistance provided in small and microenterprise development appears promising.[12]

Notes

1. Donella Meadows et al., *The Limits to Growth: A Report for the Club of Rome to Project on the Predicament of Mankind* (New York: Universe Books, 1972).

2. Thomas R. de Gregori, *A Theory of Technology* (Ames, Iowa: Iowa State University Press, 1985).

3. For a review of the literature and an extended discussion of the issues see: Colclough (1989), cited in Kaplinsky, *The Economies of Small: Appropriate Technology in a Changing World* (London: IT Publications, 1990).

4. Even if the U.S. economy were driven by market forces, the conditions in the United States are not replicable in most developing countries. The United States had available investment capital, natural resources and a trained labor force.

5. *Statistical Abstract of the United States* (Washington, D.C.: Government Printing Office, 1988).

6. There is suspiciously little debate about the reasons for the failure to service these loans. Was it the choice of technology, in which these countries decided to invest their rather easily obtained foreign currencies, followed by the failure of these large-scale industries to generate enough revenue to pay back the loans?

7. G. A. Cornia, R. Jolly and F. Stewart, *Adjustment with a Human Face* (Oxford: Oxford University Press, 1987).

8. Cornia, Jolly and Stewart, p. 67.

9. Cornia, Jolly and Stewart, p. 67.

10. Cornia, Jolly and Stewart, p. 69.

11. Statement made by U.S. Secretary of State James Baker at the inauguration of the Deputy Administrator of the U. S. Agency for International Development, Edelman, August 1989.

12. In Francis Stewart, Henk Thomas and Ton de Wilde, *The Other Policy: The Influence of*

Policies on Technology Choice and Small Enterprise Development (London: IT Publications, 1990).

13. During the period 1984–1987, Appropriate Technology International used some type of consumption financing to create markets for the products of more than 1,200 microenterprises. As of the end of 1988, more than 75 percent of these businesses were still operating and showed a positive cash flow.

1 Supply-Side Interventions: A Summary of Failures in Support of Small-Scale Enterprise

THE TARGET GROUP for programs in support of small-scale income-generating activities is large. Not counting the people who live in the nineteen industrially advanced countries (IACs), more than 3.9 billion people live in the rest of the world. Sixty-three percent of these (2.4 billion) live in rural areas. Of these rural inhabitants, 25 percent earn an income from non-farm activities; 10 percent of all rural inhabitants are employed in manufacturing activities.

Recent studies point out that the share of total manufacturing employment located in rural areas decreases with the degree of a country's industrialization and development.[1] The rural share of total manufacturing employment ranges from 65 percent to 85 percent in the least industrialized countries to 45 percent to 60 percent in the somewhat more industrialized countries of India and Pakistan. But the people who do not have access to markets—those who live and work in the informal sector—are not included in most of these statistics, although these people contribute significantly to national economic activities. Hernando de Soto shows that more than 48 percent of the work in Peru takes place in the informal sector and contributes more than 38 percent of the gross domestic product (GDP). Projections for the year 2000 estimate that these informal activities will account for more than 61 percent of the Peruvian GDP. De Soto's study of legality in the business, manufacturing, housing and transportation area shows that in Lima alone, the black market (excluding manufacture) employs 439,000 people.[2] Ninety-five percent of public transportation belongs to the black marketeers, who have invested more than US$1 billion in vehicles and vehicle maintenance. Housing figures are equally impressive. Half the population of Lima lives in houses built by the informal sector. Between 1960 and 1984, the state constructed low-income housing at a cost of US$174 million. During the same period, the black marketeers managed to construct housing valued at the inconceivable figure of US$8.3 billion, forty-seven times the amount spent by the official state.

Supply-Side Interventions: Support for Large-Scale Industries

Supply-side interventions can be divided into two categories: support for large-scale industries and support for small-scale income-generating programs. Unfortunately, a wide array of policies and procedures instituted by governments to support large-scale, capital-intensive industry have resulted in a hostile policy environment for small-scale, rural-based industry. The next section describes some of these policies and how they affected the small-scale sector.

Taxation and Investment Promotion Policies— Only for the Large-Scale Urban Enterprises

Tax credit schemes designed to promote investment, such as subsidies, special credit allowances and tax holidays, provided cheap credit and fewer costs for large firms. For example, in Thailand investment incentives were introduced by the Board of Investment in 1960. Benefits consisted of guarantees (for example, against nationalization and competition from state enterprises); special permissions (to bring in foreign staff, own land, repatriate profits); protection (import bans and surcharges against foreign competition, and tariff relief on imports); and tax incentives (exceptions from corporate income tax and other taxes). Board requirements on minimum size and capital investment deprived small firms of these privileges; in fact, the larger the firm, the longer the tax holiday. The researcher who studied the interaction between these policies and the effect on technology choice and small-scale enterprise development concluded the following:

The overall cost reduction of the promotion policies were 34.6 percent for the intermediate technology and 38.7 percent for the semi-advanced. Nonpromoted firms, which included almost all small firms, were thereby heavily penalized.[3]

In the Philippines, the Investment Incentives Act of 1967 and the Export Incentives Act of 1970 contained a package of fiscal incentives for manufacturing enterprises registered with the Board of Investment (BOI). To register with the BOI, the enterprise had to provide audited statements of accounts and other official documents; this rule made it virtually impossible for a small, rural-based entrepreneur, situated outside Metro Manila, to register. Among the incentives received by the few, mainly large, firms registered with the BOI were the following:

- Tax exemption on imported capital acquired within seven years from the date of registration of the company
- Tax credit on domestic capital equipment equivalent to 100 percent of customs duties
- Tax deduction of expansion reinvestment
- Preferential access to low-interest credit

The above measures distorted the price of capital for the small firms by more than 50 to 100 percent.

Expensive Credit for the Small Entrepreneur

Limited access to credit and the high cost of credit are two major factors with which the small-scale entrepreneur must contend. Traditional forms of credit require substantial collateral, well-established accounting procedures and guarantees that most small-scale entrepreneurs cannot provide. These obstacles partly explain why only 1 to 2 percent of the microenterprises in rural areas avail themselves of formal credit. The differences in cost of capital between the formal and informal credit market are astronomical, as can be seen in Table 1-1. According to a 1975 survey,[4] in two-thirds of developing countries, nominal interest rates in the formal sector were 10 percent or less. In contrast, interest rates in the informal sector often exceed 100 percent per annum.

Table 1-1 Real Interest Rates per Annum for Selected Countries

Country	Informal Sector	Formal Sector
Nigeria	192	-2
Ivory Coast	145	6
Sudan	120	7
Bolivia	96	5
Ethiopia	66	8
Ghana	64	0
Sierra Leone	60	-3
Malaysia	58	16
Mexico	57	7
Chile	52	-16
South Korea	49	5
Colombia	40	16
Brazil	38	-7
Honduras	37	6
Indonesia	29	3
Pakistan	27	4
Costa Rica	20	4
Sri Lanka	20	-1
India	15	-1

Source: From Steve Haggblade, Carl Liedholm and Donald C. Mead. "The Effect of Policy and Policy Reforms on Non-Agricultural Enterprises and Employment in Developing Countries: A Review of Past Experiences," in Stewart et al., *The Other Policy* (London: IT Publications, 1990).

In an extensive study of more than 21,000 small enterprises in more than twenty countries, Liedholm and Mead found that, in general, the cost of capital is the most distorted factor of production. On average, small-scale enterprises pay 40 to 60 percent more for capital than do large firms.[5]

Unequal Competition: Parastatals and Product Policies

Many countries require that all produce be processed by parastatals established for that purpose. When the government of Zimbabwe changed its policy to permit small-scale manual processing of sunflower seeds into oil (mainly used for cooking), the consumer price of oil decreased by two-thirds.[6]

In general, accounting systems of parastatals do not include depreciation expenses for machinery and equipment, although a private entrepreneur who wants to stay in business for more than a couple of years regards depreciation as an essential expense. As a result, parastatals can sell their products at a lower cost per unit than private industry. Kaplinsky, in a comparison of small-scale versus large-scale technology in sugar manufacturing in Kenya, showed that as a result of the differences in accounting practices, production cost per ton of sugar in the large-scale government-controlled industry was calculated as KSh193 per ton; the private sector that depreciated its equipment could produce sugar for KSh190.[7] If parastatals and the private sector had used the same accounting method (which included the depreciation expense), the parastatals' production cost per ton of sugar would have been KSh287. Table 1-2 compares cost and employment in the hypothetical situation where all sugar in Kenya is processed in large-scale plants with cost and employment all sugar is processed in small-scale units.

Table 1-2   Capital and Labor Utilization and Number of Sugar Processing Plants Required to Achieve 1982 Production Levels in Kenya (380,000 tons)

	No. of Plants	Capital Cost (KSh)	Employment
Large scale	2.6	338	4,420
Small scale	81	91	25,920

Source: R. Kaplinsky. *The Economies of Small: Appropriate Technology in a Changing World* (London: IT Publications, 1990).

Many governments have invested in production facilities that introduce a higher quality product that often competes with a lower quality product produced by the small-scale sector in rural areas. The desire to sustain high standards of product quality was the justification for the capital-intensive choice of technology in a large number of import substitution industries, where small-scale, commercially viable alternatives were available. For example, to satisfy only a very small market of high-income consumers, a large-scale, capital-intensive grain mill was established in Tanzania; this has put many small-scale mills out of business.[8]

Examples of more profitable small-scale alternatives include production of laundry detergent, bread, oil processing, printing ink, cement, maize milling and beer. Governments, with the involvement of bi- and multi-national donor agencies, often incorrectly claim that capital-intensive techniques are required to produce for export. This was the justification used to explain the choice of a sophisticated rice mill in the Philippines, and the rather advanced technology chosen for a shoe factory in Tanzania.[9] In these cases, high quality was used as a competitive device instead of low price. In neither case, in fact, did exports materialize.

Research and Development

Until recently, students of polytechnics in Kenya were taught to calculate the strength of support for electric wire by using the example of snow load. This is typical of the inappropriate practices in educational science and technology development programs. Many of the international agricultural research institutes and national research institutes in Third World countries spend scarce resources to improve the efficiency of resources owned by the rich, and neglect to assist in improving the resources and technology of the poor. For example, in the early 1970s, one Latin American country spent 90 percent of its research & development budget to improve productivity of crops under irrigation. But only 6 percent of that country's arable land was irrigated. Thus, only 10 percent of R&D was devoted to improve production methods for 94 percent of the land.

Countries that receive most of their foreign exchange from traditional export crops such as coffee, tea, rubber and cocoa tend to support special research institutes for these crops. Such crops are usually cultivated by large companies or landowners. On the other hand, minimal attention is paid to the crops grown by the very poor and small holders. For example, the Sri Lankan government invested considerable funds in rubber and tea research institutes, but it allocated only minimal resources to the research institute for spices (officially called the Institute for Minor Export Crops). In addition, it assigned only five agricultural extension officers, out of a total of several thousand, to the improvement of spice cultivation. More than 40 percent of the spices exported from Sri Lanka are produced in the backyards of the very small farmers.

Policy studies commissioned by Appropriate Technology International (ATI) that examined the factors that inhibited the development of the small-scale sector led to the conclusion that, generally, R&D efforts are concentrated in large firms, or on large-scale or inappropriate technologies in the public sector.[10]

Other Factors Creating a Hostile
Environment for Small-Scale Entrepreneurs

The small-scale entrepreneur is confronted by a number of other policies that add to a hostile environment. Although detailed information is given in other publications,[11] two of these policies are discussed here.

The first factor is the tying of foreign assistance. Is foreign assistance given to help countries, or is it given in the economic interests of the donor country? Organization for Economic Cooperation and Development (OECD) sources state that as much as 70 percent of the resources allocated for foreign assistance actually are spent in the donor countries.[12] As a result, the goods and services that small-scale enterprises in developing countries could provide are imported from the donor country instead of being procured from the small-scale enterprises in the host nation.

A second adverse factor is the lack of foreign exchange allocated to the small-scale sector. Although the need for foreign exchange in the small-scale sector is limited, some foreign exchange is required to import spare parts, such as ball bearings, or small hand tools, which can greatly improve productivity. Both in countries with administrative mechanisms to allocate foreign exchange and in countries with a market mechanism for that purpose, the small-scale sector is discriminated against.[13]

Supply-Side Interventions: Support for Small-Scale Enterprises

Supply-side interventions to support the small-scale sector can take a variety of forms such as providing training and education, setting up marketing and raw-material supply schemes, establishing industrial estates or common service facilities, establishing general purpose small industrial development agencies (SMIDAs) and, of course, providing credit and other financial services.

Training and Education Programs

Overall, training efforts can be classified into two broad categories: either NGO- or government-initiated programs. The latter are often supported by one of the United Nations agencies, or through a bilateral agreement with a government of an industrialized country. Despite good intentions, training and education programs for rural small-scale enterprises have, in general, been unsuccessful. Many NGO efforts are ineffective primarily because of lack of funds: Courses are too short, or centers have too few facilities to be of any significant use to trainees.

Although NGOs do understand the needs of the trainees, they lack the professional expertise to put forth a serious effort in the training area. For example, the Sarvodaya Shramadana Movement in Sri Lanka has a mixed record. In the traditional art of preparing handmade batik wall hangings, it might be considered the training center par excellence. A number of its trainees, after leaving the movement, have started batik production centers located in rural areas, with impressive exports and sales to the tourist industry. On the other hand, although at one time Sarvodaya operated more than twenty-three underequipped training centers for carpenters, few of the thousands of trainees learned any actual carpentry techniques or any business skills needed to operate such a business.

Government-supported programs often use unnecessarily sophisticated, overequipped training centers and workshops. A study that analyzed fifty-six rural small industrial enterprise (RSIE) programs in twenty countries commented,

> Formal programs only offer introductory vocational courses at training centers. They either deliberately eschew or fail to attract trainees from existing small industrial enterprise and RSIEs, concentrating instead on young labor-market entrants. Training is often given in overequipped centers in urban locations to trainees who have no relation with or motivation to set up a small-scale, rural-based enterprise.[14]

Industrial Estates and Common Service Facilities

Governments establish industrial estates to provide small enterprises the access to services they need in the production process but cannot afford on an individual basis. Services include utilities such as electricity and water supply as well as those needed in the actual production process, for example, welding equipment or a lathe. In theory, the estates should benefit from economies of scale.

To a politician, an industrial estate is a symbol of importance, similar to a large factory, that shows off what he or she has accomplished for the electorate. Unfortunately, the concept has a long history of failed effectiveness.[15] Other than the public festivities held in connection with the opening of the industrial estate, few members of the electorate will see any actual benefits from the investment. Of course, there are some exceptions, especially if the estate serves large- or even medium-sized cities. Generally, industrial estates do not meet the needs of small entrepreneurs. Conceptual mistakes are related to the physical structures: High masonry walls and heavily reinforced concrete floors do not provide the flexibility that small and microenterprises need to make optimal use of their space. Because of inconsistencies in the conception of the estate, selecting a location is very difficult. To serve rural-based enterprises, the estates need to be in rural areas, but they must also provide access to markets, which usually are located in urban areas. Many estates lack transportation to bring goods from the estate to the market.

Another problem lies in the fact that estates often are managed by government bureaucracies. Small- and medium-scale enterprises located just outside the estates (albeit because of the establishment of the estate) often have better access to utilities than do the enterprises in the estates. If an electric transformer fails, the entrepreneur outside the estate can immediately call the power company to get it repaired. The entrepreneur within the estate first has to contact the estate manager, who must then request permission from headquarters before phoning for repair.

Small Industrial Development Agencies (SMIDAs)

As part of their efforts to support small-scale industrialization, most governments have established small-scale industrial development agencies (SMIDAs).

These take different institutional and organizational forms. They can be parastatals, such as the Small Industry Development Organization (SIDO) in Tanzania and Zambia, or they can be part of the ministry of industry, such as the Small Industry Support Program (BIPIK) in Indonesia and the Industrial Development Board in Sri Lanka. The type of program varies from country to country, but most programs include one or two of the following: training centers and programs, technical service facilities, credit schemes, research programs and, sometimes, marketing and advertising services and the management of industrial estates. Evaluation reports of the SMIDAs indicate that overall they do not respond to the needs of the small and micro-entrepreneur, but rather serve as a training center for civil servants who want to test out the ideas they have formulated while being educated overseas. The general bureaucratic nature of SMIDAs, which lack performance criteria such as commercial viability or motivational incentives tied to the success of the programs, does not contribute to their effectiveness.

Financial Services and Provision of Credit

Because of the recent interest in small enterprises as a potential vehicle for economic growth, more and more experiences on this topic have come to light.[16] A brief overview of the general experience, especially concerning government-initiated programs, follows. It distinguishes three vehicles through which financial services are provided: formal banks, savings and loan associations and non-financial institutions such as NGOs and SMIDAs.

Formal Banks. Formal banks appear to be the least effective in providing credit to small rural enterprises. The case studies presented in Chapters 2 through 7 include descriptions of attempts by local implementing organizations to secure credit from local banks. Most banks treat small rural enterprises as miniature versions of large enterprises. Banks do not usually consider the fact that the location of an enterprise has a profound effect on its operations, nor do they appear to be eager to serve rural areas. In general, because of regulations—those of the central bank or the government, or those imposed by the bank itself— secure collateral is required. In addition, the records and guarantees that the banks require generally can be provided only by companies with large overheads.[17]

There are some exceptions. The Central Bank of Sri Lanka started a regional rural banking scheme in an effort to reach and provide better services to rural entrepreneurs, and the State Bank of Ghana, in an effort to serve the rural areas, made its banking officers mobile. The People's Bank of Indonesia, which is profitable and expanding, is another exception. Although it is a state bank, its credit program is not a traditional one. It is a vast savings and loan program, administered through 2,000 rural-based bank branches, with 4 million small savers and 1.3 million small borrowers. In addition, arrears are low, about 3 percent.

Savings and Loan Associations. Although in the formal sector it is possible to clearly distinguish between official savings and loan associations and financial programs operated by nonfinancial institutions, such a distinction is usually not possible in the rural and informal sectors. Many formal and informal sector savings and loan associations began as death aid societies to provide a decent burial for a member and his or her family.

According to available data, only a few savings and loans associations have effectively provided credit to local small-scale enterprises. By and large, the more successful efforts have been affiliated with organizations that had larger developmental objectives, such as the Mondragon Cooperative in Spain and the Sarvodaya Shramadana Movement in Sri Lanka. Mondragon is a large cooperative employing more than 12,000 workers, in manufacturing activities ranging from the production of refrigerators to small household appliances such as can openers. In the early 1980s, more than 150,000 people had savings accounts at the savings and loan association operated by the Sarvodaya Shramadana Movement. Although most of the S&L's money was invested in certificates of deposit, some of it was used to provide credit for local small-scale rural enterprises, such as carpentry shops, blacksmiths and metal repair shops.[18]

Nonfinancial Institutions. Small and microenterprises obtain most of their credit from nonfinancial organizations—if the entrepreneurs, their families and friends and local money lenders are defined as nonfinancial institutions. The women and men who operate their own small businesses usually finance these businesses themselves. This practice is advantageous because the entrepreneur is able to keep all profits earned on the capital, rather than pay interest to the owner of the capital; thus the income earned is more equally distributed. However, thousands of potential economic opportunities have not been explored or tapped, much less come to fruition, because the potential entrepreneur lacks access to, among other factors, appropriate credit.

Government organizations, including SMIDAs, and NGOs often institute credit programs because they are dissatisfied with the performance of formal financial institutions. As discussed earlier, SMIDAs lack the incentives needed to assist rural entrepreneurs, not only in providing general support, but also in helping them obtain access to credit. For example, Kenya Industrial Estates (KIE) administered, with mixed results, a now concluded program of 630 loans. Tanzania's SIDO, considered one of the more effective SMIDAs, managed a low-interest-rate equipment lease/purchase/loan scheme intended for rural, small industrial enterprises. But the majority of its loans went to urban-based industrial enterprises that were not financially viable. Overall, arrears on SIDO loans have been high. Because the money collected in repayments was used to pay operating expenses rather than being reloaned, the available capital was rapidly depleted. Recently, the government transferred the credit program from SIDO to the National Bank of Commerce.[19]

Nonfinancial NGOs have also developed credit programs. Because of the variety and informal nature of these efforts, it is difficult to formulate generic criteria that would lead to more successful programs in this area.

Success Stories

There are, however, an increasing number of success stories about well-administered credit programs. For example, the Grameen Bank in Bangladesh (a savings and loan association), which provides credit on the basis of a group guarantee of repayment, lends mainly for consumption purposes. In loans that average US$50–$60, the bank has a turnover equivalent of US$3 million per month. Working Women's Forum in Madras, India, is based on the principle that the group guarantees repayment. As of June 1988, Working Women's Forum had made loans to more than 62,000 women organized in groups of ten to twelve participants. The groups are taught how to manage the funds. Members help each other to repay the loans on time, because if one of the women defaults, none of the other women in her group can obtain a loan. Overall repayment rate is 96 percent without rescheduling. Women who have received and repaid two or more loans are encouraged to set up their own groups. Three-quarters of the loans go to service-sector activities, which, for example, allow a woman to buy fish from fisherpeople on the coast, transport the fish to a local market and sell them. Twenty-five percent of all loans go to microenterprises such as making paper flowers and *bedies* (Indian cigarettes).

Neither the magic of the marketplace (demand pull) nor supply-side interventions have been demonstrated as effective strategies to support sustainable small and microenterprise development programs. The case studies that follow are a combination of both. A small amount of specific technical and financial assistance helped the projects to enter the marketplace. Such a strategy might be called development of structured markets. The projects deal with finance and with technologies, but above all they deal with people.

Notes

1. Carl Liedholm and Donald C. Mead, *Small-scale Industries in Developing Countries: Empirical Evidence and Policy Implications* (Washington, D.C.: U.S. Agency for International Development, 1986).

2. Hernando de Soto, *The Other Path* (New York: Harper Collins, 1989).

3. M. Santikarn, "Macro-Policies for Appropriate Technology: Case Studies in Thailand." Paper prepared for Conference on Implications of Technology Choice on Economic Development Pataya, Thailand (Washington, D.C.: Appropriate Technology International, 1988). Mimeograph.

4. Steve Haggblade, Carl Liedholm and Donald C. Mead, "The Effect of Policy and Policy Reforms on Non-Agricultural Enterprises and Employment in Developing Countries: A Review of Past Experiences," in Stewart et al., *The Other Policy, The Influence of Policies on Technology Choice and Small Enterprise Development* (London: IT Publications, 1990).

5. Carl Liedholm and Donald C. Mead, *Small-Scale Industries in Developing Countries: Empirical Evidence and Policy Implications* (East Lansing: Michigan State Uni-

versity, Working Paper No. 9, Mimeograph, 1987).

6. The story on Zimbabwe is taken from J. F. Swartzendruber, "Changing Policy in Zimbabwe: Sunflower Seed Press," in *Appropriate Technology International 1987 Annual Report* (Washington, D.C.: Appropriate Technology International, 1988).

7. R. Kaplinsky, "Sugar Processing in India and Kenya," paper presented at the Nairobi Conference on Macro Policies and Impact on Technology Choice and Small Scale Enterprise Development, (Washington, D.C.: Appropriate Technology International, 1988). Mimeograph.

8. M. S. D. Bagachwa, "Technology Choice in Industry: A Study of Grain Milling Techniques in Tanzania," paper presented at the 1988 International Conference on Implications of Technology Choice on Economic Development, Nairobi, Kenya, 29–31 August, (Washington, D.C.: Appropriate Technology International, 1988). Mimeograph.

9. This example (cited in Stewart et al., *The Other Policy,* p. 30) quotes the World Bank Appraisal Report of this project as stating: "One fairly modern shoe factory presently produces leather and canvas shoes for the internal market. The output is of acceptable quality within Tanzania, but does not meet international standards. The new shoe factory . . . would produce about four million pairs of shoes to international standards, primarily for export, but it is expected that a small part of the production will be sold internally."

10. Stewart et al., p. 24.

11. Stewart et al., p. 25.

12. Organization for Economic Cooperation and Development, *DAC Report,* 1988.

13. For detailed information see M. S. D. Bagachwa (1988) and S. M. Wangwe and M. S. D. Bagachwa ("Impact of Economic Policies on Technological Choice and Development in Tanzanian Industry," 1988, in Stewart et al., *The Other Policy*). They write: "Because of their political and economic power, parastatal enterprises have been receiving a disproportionate share of allocations of foreign exchange . . . " In Zimbabwe it was noted that "bureaucratic procedures and allocation criteria tend to favor large and established firms and discriminate against the small sector" (Ndlela, 1990). In Zambia and Ghana, where administrative allocation of foreign exchange auctions, the result was the same: "The main beneficiaries were the multinational companies and the parastatals" (Ncube, 1987).

14. J. Keddie, R. Nanjudan and R. Tezler, *Development of Rural Small Industrial Enterprise: Lessons from Experience* (Vienna: United Nations Industrial Development Organization, 1988.)

15. United Nations Publications, *The Effectiveness of Industrial Estates in Developing Countries,* and *RSIE Study,* pp. 66–67.

16. See papers presented at the Seminar on Informal Financial Markets in Development," sponsored by Ohio State University, U.S. Agency for International Development and the World Bank, October 18-20, 1989, Washington, D.C.

17. The RSIE study reported that in Senegal the banks have made few small-industrial-enterprise or RSIE loans. In Kenya, Tanzania and Zambia, none of the commercial and large development banks had made loans to rural small enterprises. In each of these countries, however, small finance companies Small-Scale Enterprise Promotion Ltd. in Zambia, Small Enterprise Finance Corporation in Kenya and Cooperative and Rural Development Bank in Tanzania have made some loans to small enterprises. The majority of these small enterprises have been located in urban areas.

18. The RSIE study says that the savings and loan associations "show more promise, although their widespread effectiveness for RSIE remains unproven." Although evidence pointed out the weaknesses of rural savings and loan associations in Pakistan, Senegal and the Philippines, the study did cite two promising examples—the Credit Union and Savings Association (CUSA) in Zambia, and the Grameen Bank in Bang-

ladesh. But neither of these two institutions serves rural and informal productive small-scale enterprises. CUSA serves farmers.

19. See Chapter 4 on Tanzania.

2 Marketing of Small-scale Maize Mills in Cameroon

SEVEN YEARS AGO, JULIE MYKHAN helped create the Kong Mission Women's Group to serve the needs of the women in the Mission district of Santa in the North West Province. Now she is the Group secretary. "We realized we women needed to work together to help each other, if we were ever going to improve our lives," she explains. The Group raises corn, Irish potatoes, leeks and vegetables on a fifty-hectare farm; earnings are divided equally among the forty-eight members to be used for individual needs.

For at least a year, the Group looked for a business investment that would bring in a regular income without requiring a lot of time and attention. Six months ago, the Group signed a lease/purchase agreement to purchase the Cameroon Agricultural Tools Manufacturing Industry (CATMI) maize mill. Julie says that because they were able to buy the mill on credit, they did not investigate any alternative mills or compare prices. "We just put in our application and hoped that we would qualify," she says.

So far, the forty-eight members have been very happy with the earnings from the maize mill, which will be shared among all the members—similar to the way in which farm income is distributed. Julie expects she will use her earnings to purchase books or uniforms for her two school-age children. (A

This chapter was researched and written by Arleen Richman in association with Ton de Wilde.

third child is an infant.) The mill operates on demand; it is run by a young man, who lives on the premises.

Members of the Kong Mission Group feel that the quality of the maize flour ground by their mill is finer than the flour ground at the nearest maize mill, which is five km away. They claim their mill is drawing customers from a fifteen km range. Although taro, rather than corn, is the staple crop in this area—"every compound in the area now is cooking *foo-foo* every day," says Julie. "Our families are happier because they are eating better (*foo-foo* every day in addition to taro) and they eat on time."

Julie and the Group's other officers smile as they watch the mill operator start the engine. "Listen to that sound—we have an investment that advertises itself. People hear the mill and they come—we don't have to do anything else. We are very fortunate."

Maize is a major food crop throughout much of Cameroon and a staple in the North West Province. The Foreign Agricultural Service of the U.S. Department of Agriculture estimates that, in 1986–1987, 430,000 metric tons of maize were harvested in Cameroon. More than 40 percent of this corn was produced in the North West Province. Approximately 80 percent of the maize produced in Cameroon is for personal household consumption (subsistence); 20 percent is sold in the cities or local village markets.[1]

In parts of the North West Province, where the traditional dish called *foo-foo* (a corn porridge) is the preferred staple, it provides almost the entire diet of the rural poor. As one farmer explained, "If you are in our village and they give you any type of food without also giving you *foo-foo*, they haven't treated you well."

Fifty-eight percent of Cameroon's ten million population live in rural areas and still depend on agriculture for subsistence.[2] A favorable climate allows a wide variety of crops, fruits and vegetables to be grown. The climate in the North West Province, of which Bamenda is the capital, is ideal for maize cultivation. Most of the province is high-plateau; Bamenda itself is at an altitude of 1,219 meters and is ringed by mountains reaching a height of 2,743 meters.

The Production of Maize

Throughout Cameroon, maize almost always is grown by women. Men plant cash crops such as coffee and cotton. Women labor on their husbands' farms and work even harder on their own plots to produce corn, beans, coco yams and cassava. Women also grow maize on communal farms maintained by their association. Most of the food they produce is consumed by their families; however, they sell at local markets any food not needed for subsistence.

Introduction of Mechanized Milling

Traditionally, maize was ground by hand. Women would put the corn on a hardstone table and crush it with a stone roller. Just to grind enough corn for one family's meals took almost two and a half hours each day.

In the early 1950s, a local trader introduced the first handmill into the North West Province; he charged a small amount to grind a small basket of grain—approximately 3 kilograms (kg) or one day's meals for a family. Hand-operated maize mills can process approximately 16 to 18 kilograms (kg) of corn per hour. To compute the time necessary to obtain the ground maize flour, however, one should add the time it takes to walk to the mill, wait in line and walk back home. Nevertheless, the mill reduced labor time significantly.

The cost of the mill prevented its widespread use. Although handmills are relatively less expensive today (1988 prices ranged from US$300 to $650), given a choice most people prefer motor-driven plate mills.

Plate mills grind the corn through the friction between two round plates that move against each other. Hammer mills grind corn by small mechanically driven metal hammers that hit the corn against a metal sieve.

The Introduction of Motorized Mills

In the early 1960s, the first imported diesel-powered plate mills were installed in urban centers of areas where maize production was abundant. Because these new machines reduced labor significantly without destroying the meal's flavor, people clearly preferred them. Service was faster, for now it took less than two minutes to mill the 3 kg of maize required for a family's daily meals.

The expensive mills were difficult to maintain. Replacement parts were not readily available and there were few mechanics trained to repair and maintain the mills. Hence, many mills experienced considerable downtime. Although the majority of the users of these service mills were rural, low-income households, generally only established businessmen and some wealthy farmers could afford to purchase them.

The Economic Impact of Small-Scale Maize Milling Units

Recent studies regarding the choice of technology, affirmed by empirical evidence, indicate that if all families were provided access to maize milling equipment, the time saved would be used to add income to their subsistence-level existence. A recent International Labor Organization (ILO) study on food processing in Africa found that "when power operated equipment to replace time and/or energy consuming tasks becomes available through payment of rental fees, rural women allocate money to purchase these services indicating a strong willingness to pay in order to free time."[3] A later survey by the United Nations Development Fund for Women (UNIFEM) on the role of women and technology indicates that part of the time gained by using the labor-saving devices is devoted to intensifying farming activities and generating income.[4] An informal survey of ten women in the villages of Oku and Ndu conducted by an Appropriate Technology International (ATI) project officer in 1986 corroborated these findings.[5] Ninety percent of the respondents using mechanized mills stated that they devoted most of the time they saved to farming and marketing activities.

In Cameroon, as in many other countries in West Africa, the role of women and men in the economy varies depending on such factors as ethnic group and religion. In most groups, marketing of cash crops is a male activity and cultivation of food crops, such as maize, is women's work. Women in these groups do market their excess household production and control the money they earn in this manner. Women sell excess household garden production—corn, Irish potatoes and cabbages—at specified times in order to raise money for school fees or special household emergencies. In a few areas, because of different ethnic customs, women do not have control over any earned money; all money is immediately turned over to the male head of their household unit.

In another survey, members of women's groups who had recently obtained maize mills and people living near the mills were interviewed.[6] Near Fundong, in the North West Province, where coffee is the major cash crop, several coffee farmers were enthusiastic about the maize mills' potential economic benefits—both for the individual farmers and for the town. Previously, the women of Fundong had to walk forty-five minutes each way to have their corn ground. The women and the men agreed that the women would use most of this newly found time to help plant more coffee. The vice president of the local branch of the coffee cooperative estimated that, in two years, the additional land the women would be able to plant with coffee should result in an anticipated harvest per average farm family of seven bags of coffee compared to the current five bags. Coffee of the quality produced in this area was selling for 19,000 Cameroon francs (CFA) per bag in August 1988. At the exchange rate of CFA300 per US$1, the additional harvest represents an annual increase in cash income of US$127 per coffee farmer.

Another group near Santa, whose members were not involved in raising coffee and who lived in an area where corn is a secondary crop, estimated that just by using the time saved in going to a mill, each member could plant, harvest, and sell annually the equivalent of three buckets of corn; this realized additional income of approximately US$6 per year per member. Any remaining "saved" time was expected to be used to grow additional vegetables on the group farm. Interviews with members of three other groups elicited similar information.

Clearly, mechanizing women's laborious tasks, such as grinding corn, gives them time that they can devote to income-generating activities. These findings corroborated findings published in the UNIFEM paper of studies from the Philippines and other countries, which suggest that "technologies which increase labor productivity in non-farm activities could well allow women to maintain levels of personal income at the same time as being able to give more attention to food production and preparation, child care, etc."[7]

The Historical Role of Women's Associations in Cameroon

Because preparation of maize flour has always played a central role in women's lives, it is not surprising to learn that the first women's organizations in

Cameroon were corn-milling societies.

In the early 1950s, Elizabeth O'Kelly, a British community organizer and social worker, wanted to bring women together so that they could attend literacy classes, learn food preparation, nutrition and child-care techniques and become familiar with improved agricultural practices. Because the women were occupied from sunrise to sunset with traditional women's activities (growing food crops, caring for children and preparing meals, including grinding corn), they had no free time to better the quality of their life. To lighten the women's labor and to create a focal point around which societies could be formed, she introduced hand-driven maize mills in North West Cameroon.[8] The mills were owned and operated by the women as a group. Once the women banded together, they could be taught reading and writing as well as other skills, such as soap making. The corn mill societies appeared in numerous villages, and some societies undertook other activities such as savings clubs and maintenance of communal group farms.

Initially, O'Kelly obtained a grant from the Ministry of Education to set up a revolving loan fund to import ten mills from England. The women's groups had to pay for the mills within two years of receipt. They earned the money by charging a fee for the ground corn (although some groups simply charged each woman who used the mill a monthly fee), by farming land collectively as the society's farm and selling the produce and by selling homemade baskets or pots. Remarkably, over an eight-year period, there were no bad debts.

Word of the corn mill societies spread rapidly until more than 300 mills had been purchased and installed. At their peak in 1959, the corn mill societies had a total membership of more than 30,000 women; groups had spread even to coastal areas and had cut across ethnic boundaries.

When O'Kelly left Cameroon in the early 1960s, the groups began to disband. By the early 1970s, few corn societies remained. A recent report attributes their decline to their inability to increase the functions of the organizations, the lack of cooperative education and the inability of the members to locate spare parts for the mills, which had become obsolete.[9]

In the 1970s some of the dormant corn societies were rejuvenated as women's cooperatives, often connected to a male-dominated union, to market cash crops. The coffee marketing cooperatives did attempt to re-introduce corn mills as a male-dominated cooperative activity in areas where large amounts of corn were grown. Because their activities were not well supervised, however, the motorized cooperative corn mills were not very profitable. Replacement parts for the imported mills were still difficult to obtain and eventually most of the cooperative corn mills were also abandoned.

Women's Cooperative Societies Today

A few corn societies that can trace their origin to the original O'Kelly corn societies continue to operate maize mills and to operate communal farms, although some of these have substantially diversified their activities. Current cooperative societies generally center around cooperative shops and/or the marketing of members' produce. Some larger societies buy and sell palm oil—mostly for their members' use. Cooperative members receive training in simple management and bookkeeping techniques.

In addition to the formal women's cooperatives, numerous informal women's groups exist. Members generally have a common purpose and are organized to carry out cultural, religious or neighborhood activities. In the 1980s, the North West Province Development Authority (MIDENO), began to structure these groups into associations; as more formal organizations, they could be used as vehicles for the extension of rural credit.

To qualify as a Food Crop Group association, a group must: be in existence for a number of years and have a respected leadership; be manageable in size—no more than fifty members; receive agricultural extension services; and have received training in credit practices. MIDENO records show twenty-three such Women's Food Crop Groups with 474 members in 1984–1985; by 1987–1988, 10,754 women belonged to 363 Food Crop Groups.

These groups, many of which operate communal farms, are constantly seeking income-generating activities. If a way could be found to finance the purchase of a maize mill by the Food Crop Groups and the more formally organized women's associations, a primary market for the ATI-CATMI maize mill could be created.

Demand and Its Obstacles

Although milling services are common in Cameroon's urban areas and market towns, when the maize mill project began in 1985 there was no market for maize mills in the rural areas where the actual maize producers and consumers lived. Demand for the services and demand for income-generating activities certainly existed. But the rural poor did not have access to credit to enable them to purchase the mills. And, if by chance, a rural farmer was able to buy an imported mill, how could he or she obtain the replacement parts to keep the mill running so that it could generate a reliable income?

These limitations did not prevent wealthier urban-based entrepreneurs and businessmen from buying maize mills. Sales figures for the period 1979-1984 obtained by Association for the Promotion of Community Initiatives in Africa (APICA), the implementing organization for the maize mill project, describe the market for sixteen types of maize mills, ranging in capacity from 7 kg/hr to 9 kg/hr for a manual mill to as high as 450 kg/hr for an imported mechanized plate mill. Total sales for both hand- and machine-driven mills in Cameroon are shown in Table 2-1.

In five years, 2,368 maize mills of various types were sold in Cameroon. The upward trend in sales figures was confirmed in an interview conducted in 1988 with Jean Sangou, spokesman for R. W. King, the largest wholesale and retail distributor of imported mills in the Douala area.

Sangou classified retail buyers into two groups: those who buy the mills to set up a milling service (investment) and a few private citizens who buy small handmills for their own convenient home use. Differences in prices of the same mill offered by wholesalers generally can be attributed to inclusion or omission of maintenance services and guaranteed part replacement.

Table 2-1   Total Sales for Hand- and Machine-Driven Mills in Cameroon.

Year	Sales
1979–1980	458
1980–1981	460
1981–1982	475
1982–1983	390
1983–1984	585

Although taking corn to the mill was certainly less tedious and monotonous than pounding it by hand, women still had to spend many hours traveling to and from the service mills. A survey conducted by Jean Bosco Toukam, a development official with APICA, in 1985 revealed that, in the North West Province, women traveled as far as 10 km on foot and, on occasion, 20 km by truck to have their maize ground. Usually these long trips would be made on market day. An informal survey indicated that in 1984 women traveled by foot an average of 1.2 km each way to have their maize ground—a total walk of forty-five minutes. And they did this at least four times per week.[10]

Methods of Production

Hand Pounding

In 1985, approximately 60 percent of maize in Cameroon was processed by mechanized grain mills, 10 percent by handmills and 30 percent by traditional hand-grinding.[11] Pounding corn in the traditional manner is still practiced in isolated areas of the North West Province. The maize is ground on a hard stone surface that is placed on the ground. The woman kneels at one end of a grindstone that is approximately 24 in. long and 16-20 in. wide; a slightly concave basket is placed at the other end to catch the flour. Using a small tortoise-shaped stone held with both hands, she rubs back and forth over the larger stone surface. It takes about one hour to grind 1 1/3 kilos of maize this way. Thus, to feed an average size family of five or six people, it takes about two and a half hours to prepare the maize flour for the day.

Hand-Operated Grain Mills

Hand-operated mills were very popular when they first appeared in Cameroon in the early 1950s because they did save time and energy compared to the traditional process. Today they are used only in areas where there are no motorized mills or in an emergency or as a last resort in areas where milling services exist. In Cameroon's capital, Douala, no one who was questioned could name any handmill that was still being operated as a service mill.

Although handmilling services do exist in the Bamenda area, they are at best a poor second choice. People who have used them complain they require almost as much time and energy as the traditional method. Toukam claims that children associate the milling method a family uses with "a degree of comfort enjoyed by the family." If handmills and motor mills are equally accessible, a family who has the extra cash to pay for the faster service would certainly do so. Toukam recalled that "in 1975 when my mother asked me to help her grind corn on our handmill, I asked her why she wouldn't send me to the motorized mill, since we did have the money to pay for the service."

The Missing Factors:
A Locally Produced Mill and Credit for Local Groups

Because most users already were familiar with motorized maize mills, only two factors were necessary to improve the productivity of maize milling: mills, which could be produced locally and for which spare parts were readily accessible in the country; and credit so that users, either individuals or associations, could purchase these mills.

Local Production of a Plate Mill

To overcome the first problem, APICA, ATI and B. A. Anguh, owner of a machine shop that produced coffee pulpers and other agricultural implements, studied the possibility of producing a maize plate mill locally. The ATI-supported plate mill is similar to the principal imported model with which it competes. Production of this mill started in early 1988. Components of the adapted mill have been redesigned to be made from mild steel plate, sheet and angle bars. Only bearings, grinding plates and springs need to be imported. Initially, the adapted maize mill cost 20 percent less than the imported model.[12]

The improved motor-driven mill can process 150 kg of maize each hour. Thus it can grind the 1.12 tons of maize processed annually per household in about seven and a half hours. This compares favorably with the 824 hours required using the traditional method and the sixty-two hours required using the handmill.

Commercial Viability of the Maize Mill

Local production of the plate mills solved the problem of lack of availability of imported spare parts. If the rural poor were to have access to ownership of the means of production, however, they needed credit so that they could purchase the mills. Therefore, the commercial viability of the mills needed to be assessed.

Table 2-2 and its underlying assumptions document the commercial viability of the Anguh plate mill. A key assumption supporting its commercial viability is the cost at which maize will be milled. The assessment of the Anguh Maize Mill project assumed a conservative milling charge of CFA150 per tin. At that time some local mills were charging as much as CFA250 per tin. A study of prices charged in July 1988 by four women's groups that were among the first groups to lease/purchase the mill revealed that their charges ranged from CFA125 to CFA185 per tin.[13] They also serviced smaller bucket quantities for which they charged CFA50 each. In all cases, the women's groups were charging either the same price as their closest (in distance) competitor, or a bit less. One of the groups explained that they set their price "to serve the women of the area so the women could use the service and not suffer." Because all groups voiced an intention to help their villages, members of the women's groups owning the mill were charged the same price as nonmembers.

Table 2-2   Commercial Analysis, Maize Mill Service Enterprise

Production Capacity:	147,000 kg/yr
Capital Costs in Francs CFA	
Land	12,000
Buildings	40,000
Equipment	1,353,000
Total	1,405,000
Fixed Costs in Francs CFA	
Maintenance	142,000
Salaries	72,000
Finance Costs	
Depreciation	180,000
Interest (10%)	147,000
Total Fixed Costs	541,000
Variable Costs in Francs CFA	
Energy (fuel)	449,100
Oil	36,000
Total Yearly Variable Costs	485,100

Variable Cost per Unit = Production Capacity/Variable Costs = 3.3

Milling Fee	CFA150/bucket
1 bucket	15 kg
Milling Fee per kg.	CFA10

Contribution per Unit = (Sales Price/Unit −Variable Cost/Unit) = CFA6.7

Breakeven Units	= Total Fixed Costs/Contribution/Unit
	= 80,746
Breakeven %	= 55 %

Availability of Credit

Although the commercial analysis proves that a milling operation could be profitable, a potential buyer still must have credit to purchase the mill. In-

formal lending sources traditionally used as a source of credit rarely provide more than CFA20,000 at one time. In 1989, an Anguh maize mill cost
CFA1,350,000 (US$4,500) Where would the rural poor get the credit to pur-
chase these mills? What bank or lending institution would give them a loan? If
they were able to obtain a loan to purchase a mill, how would they be able to
maintain it in good working order so that they could continue to generate the
income necessary to keep up with the loan payments?

When some fifty members of women's societies, government and banking
officials and community organizers were asked how a small-scale rural farmer
could obtain a loan, most of them just laughed. They claimed that loans are
given only to those with political power. If you don't know someone important
in the government, they said, a bank will not even consider your application.

Banks

Spokespeople for branches of the four major banks in Bamenda, the Banque
Internationale d'Afrique Occidentale (BIAO), Cameroon Bank, the Banque
Internationale pour le Commerce et l'Industrie du Cameroun (BICIC) and the
Societe Camerounaise de Banque (SCB), acknowledge that the commercial
lending policy toward the rural sector is "very weak." The banks' lending policies are based on security and guarantees. Major collateral in Cameroon, as in
developed nations, would be title to land and property. But only about 5 percent of all owners/users of arable land under cultivation have deeds or other
proof of registration. If the farmer has no title to the land, he or she cannot
pledge the land as collateral. Overall rights to communal land use (the vast
majority of all available land) generally rest with traditional authorities and
depend on inheritance and ethnic customs. People plant as much land as they
are able to cultivate. Some portions of the crops harvested or cash earned
from the sale of the crops may be given to local traditional authorities in
exchange for use of the land.[14]

If sufficient collateral is not posted, a loan application must be guaranteed
by a civil servant or a salaried person whose wages are deposited directly into
his or her bank account. The regional manager for the Cameroon Bank stated
that fewer than 200,000 people out of Cameroon's total population of 10 million
could qualify as guarantors. (Estimates by government officials were even
lower.) Guarantors almost always have an ethnic or kinship relationship or
political connections to the loan application. Francois Tchakui of the BICIC
noted that his bank has one well-known successful businessman who is standing as guarantor for ten loans to young members of his ethnic group as they
establish their own businesses.[15] The important role of the guarantor is better
understood when one knows that 50 to 60 percent of all business loans go bad.
Tchakui attributes this to lack of planning for the business, and diversion of
funds for purposes other than the stated loan. A government official explained
that "Most of these loans are bad from the very beginning. The banks lend the
money knowing that the loans are bad, but some of the bankers are getting
kickbacks or favors or they cannot refuse because of political or tribal pres-

sure. When the loan goes bad, the banker doesn't suffer. The banker is transferred . . . like a flea jumping from dog to dog." In 1989, after three major banks were closed because of bad loans and financial mismanagement, a major reorganization of the entire banking system was instigated.

Rural villagers who do not hold title to land have very little chance of locating a guarantor. But even if they did, they probably could still not get a loan from the banks. The Cameroon Bank claims it must turn down 90 percent of all applicants because they have no cash available to loan. All bankers and public officials acknowledged that, in actuality, few funds were available for lending—one of the side effects of the recent economic recession in Cameroon exacerbated by bad loans and financial mismanagement. Because there is so little liquidity, a potential new customer—such as a rural women's group wishing to buy a maize mill that has no patron—has little chance of obtaining a loan.

In 1989, the Cameroon government owned more than 51 percent of all banks except the Cameroon Bank; 49 percent or less of the ownership of these banks was held by private parties. Interest rates are determined by the Central Bank, as are overall lending policies. Banks generally offer consumption loans for short-term purchases (television or stereo equipment) for one year; home construction loans and building loans for four to ten years; and business investment loans for one to two years. Interest rates range from 11 percent on rediscountable loans (refinanced by the Central Bank) to 18 percent for overdrafts and business loans, which the banks finance at their own risk. The Cameroon Bank stated that nationals can obtain certain types of loans for as little as 10 percent interest. The inflation rate in 1988 was approximately 10 percent.

The National Fund for Rural Development (FONADER), has long been the traditional formal avenue for loans to the rural agricultural sector and the most likely provider of a loan to a rural farmer. FONADER is now in transition; the government expects to replace it with a nationwide agricultural development bank. The activities of FONADER are restricted to recovering loans it previously made and implementing the credit activities of MIDENO.

Alexander Lantum, Credit Advisor to MIDENO, acknowledged FONADER's inability, even when it was fully functioning, to provide credit to individual small rural farmers. Although FONADER was the major source of loans to large farmers and to intermediaries such as cooperatives who would then lend to groups of small farmers, it was not established to make loans to individual small farmers.

FONADER's regulations held the group responsible for repayment; its regulations regarding collateral and guarantors were similar to those of the commercial banks. Lacking full collateral, a potential borrower must get a civil servant or a person whose salary was deposited directly to his or her bank account to sign as a guarantor. Civil servants' salaries are paid directly to their accounts in commercial banks; thus a bank could attach the salary if the loan were in default. As with commercial banks, many loans went to people who knew government officials, and many were used for purposes other than the ones stated in the loan—that is, to build a house rather than to purchase stipulated agricultural machinery. FONADER did loan to large farmers, who had collateral and title to the land, and to cooperatives. The cooperatives in turn would lend money only to farmers who had a proved or known ability to repay. Although each cooperative set its own criteria for income, production and so forth, a small farmer who sold only two bags of coffee per year could not realistically expect to qualify for any loan. The only source of credit available to the small-scale farmer and the majority of poor rural people was the *njange*, the traditional lending group.

Traditional Lending

A *njange,* an informal lending group, exists for everyone, and it is the largest source of credit throughout Cameroon. Everyone with whom the authors of this chapter spoke—government officials, women farmers and office workers—belonged to one or more *njanges*. A women's group would most likely have a *njange*, all places of employment had a *njange* and friends often organized a *njange*. Businessmen might belong to as many as five of these informal lending groups. Groups might also be organized by social purpose: Their members gather for a party or a dinner once a month, or even once a week.

Generally there are no written rules for membership, but the members must trust one another and new members must be introduced by a present member or belong to the *njange* by virtue of becoming employed in a certain office. At each meeting, every member is required to contribute a set amount to the savings kitty, which is given to one member. After all members have had a chance to take home the pot, the *njange* is dissolved. The *njange* then begins again, perhaps with different members and a different order of distribution.

A few of the *njanges,* usually composed of the wealthier members of society, do charge interest; the interest accrued is shared among the members when the group dissolves. More sophisticated groups also may require a new member to give a signed, blank check as collateral to the *njange* secretary. Rural groups composed of farmers usually operate without any such formal structures.

Other informal groups used as intermediaries to obtain credit include lend-hand societies, cultural groups, religious groups and home economic centers.[16] Lend-hand societies where the members pool their labor to effect a particular farm operation—clearing or harvesting—have evolved into *njanges*. Savings societies, locally called Sunday meetings, operate as informal banks, usually lending money for a specific purpose, such as taxes and school fees. Business is usually conducted on Sunday. Membership in Sunday meetings is limited to a very small group of insiders. All savings, plus the interest earned, are shared at a predetermined time of year.

Membership in cultural groups is limited to extended family, clan or district. Members of religious groups and associations often wear a uniform and/or religious emblems. Church matters aside, these groups accept deposits from members, extend credit and purchase and distribute essential household commodities in bulk. Government-sponsored home economic groups receive training from the Women's Wing of the Department of Community Development in the Ministry of Agriculture; membership is open to all women in a locality.

Alexander Lantum of MIDENO explained that, with the exception of very sophisticated groups composed of the urban elite, the credit obtained through *njanges* (generally a maximum of CFA20,000) "is too small to permit any meaningful development." Although they serve a useful purpose and may be the only source of credit available to most of the rural poor, they are not a legal entity and they do not employ trained administrative staff. For several years, Lantum has been working to organize many of these informal groups, and the women's Food Crop associations, into a formal association that would be linked to a formal source of credit—a true people's bank.

Introducing the Credit Mechanism to Purchase the Mills

Although the need for locally produced maize mills was evident, an innovative financial scheme was required to create a market. ATI and APICA teamed up with MIDENO to create a project containing three major elements: the technical development, production, and maintenance of a locally produced maize mill based on Anguh's initial designs; identification and training of groups and individuals who would purchase and operate these mills; and development and implementation of an innovative financial mechanism that would give the poor majority of maize consumers access to ownership of these mills. Four groups were involved in implementing this plan. CATMI and ATI finalized the design of the mill and put it into production; MIDENO and APICA identified and trained the purchasers/users; and APICA, MIDENO and ATI developed and implemented a lease/purchase scheme, which gave women's groups access to the mills.

The Organizations

Anguh the Entrepreneur—The Idea and the Maize Mill. Anguh established CATMI in 1972 to "respond to the need for a local industry that could manufacture and repair farm and agricultural product processing equipment." Anguh, who was orphaned as a young boy and apprenticed to a village blacksmith, had begun his toolmaking in earnest in Big Babanki (a village about thirty miles from Bamenda); here he fabricated garden hand tools and knives and even experimented with designing a sewing machine. In 1962, "a year of anxiety," he began experimenting with a machine that would pulp coffee after it was harvested. His first efforts were, as he says, "sadly lacking." Because he had never had the opportunity to go to school, he was not able to calculate the measurements necessary to build the coffee pulper. Then, in 1965, at age twenty-three, he entered primary school and completed a seven-year course in four years. "It took a lot to go to school at my advanced age," he recalls, "but I knew I would remain just a village blacksmith if I could not calculate and express myself."

In 1971, he perfected his coffee pulper, which is designed to accommodate the locally grown Cameroon Arabian coffee and is the only locally manufactured machine of its kind in the country. Coffee pulpers became the mainstay of his business. Between 1975 and 1984 he produced 10,000 coffee pulpers, which he sold to cooperatives in the North West and Western Provinces. As soon as he was satisfied with the design for the coffee pulper, he began experimenting with other products. "As a businessman, I knew that it is dangerous to rely on only one product. I knew I needed to diversify my production if my business was to succeed over the long run."

He recognized a need for a maize mill. "I saw the distances women walked to have their corn ground and I knew the cost of the imported maize mills. I was convinced that a diesel-powered plate mill for maize would be useful to all my people and therefore would be something they would be willing to pay for—if I could produce a good quality product for the right price." After tinkering with various designs, in 1979, assisted by a British engineer (a Food and Agriculture Organization (FAO) consultant), he built a prototype diesel-powered maize mill based on the design for a locally available imported mill. But he was not satisfied with this prototype, or with any of the modified designs he produced later.

In 1985, ATI hired an engineer to work in Cameroon with Anguh to help him redesign the maize mill. The ATI-supported mill is similar to the principal imported diesel-powered mill with which it competes. The major difference is that the Anguh mill is built by components that are welded together. This design eliminates the need for a casted frame, which could not be produced or repaired in Cameroon.

Three design changes greatly improved the mill's performance and reliability. The frame has been modified so that the engine and mills for all diesel-powered models can be independently mounted; this change provides a more secure and vibration-free attachment for the engine. A vibrating feeder trough automatically moves the corn into the machine. This eliminates the need to shift the maize manually and prevents the trough from becoming clogged. Incorporating an appropriate perforation size screen into the hopper separates the large foreign objects and prevents children from dropping coins or other objects into it.

Production capacity of the mill has been measured at 150 kg per hour. Wet maize can be ground without jamming the machine, which saves the substantial amount of time normally wasted in drying the corn. The plate mill can be easily adjusted so that the grain can be ground the way the customer wants it.

Dimensions of parts are identical from one machine to another (within reasonable limits). This interchangeability of parts is an essential feature of quality control. Fuel consumption is less than or equivalent to that of the imported mills (the minimum possible in a mill with cast iron plates) and does not exceed 150 ml/10 kg of white maize.[17] To purchase raw materials to manufacture the first twenty mills and a stock of replacement parts necessary to begin the commercial cycle of press production and marketing, ATI provided CATMI with a working capital loan on commercial terms. This loan is expected to be repaid in five years.

The Lease/Purchase Scheme

As part of the project design, an assessment was made of the financial situation of the rural households who most needed access to milling facilities. As reported earlier, rural farmers and women's groups do not have access to conventional forms of financing. The capital required to purchase the mill is much greater than the amount of money normally provided by traditional informal lending sources. In addition, most poor rural people can afford to take only a small margin of risk. Why should they invest in a new technology about which there is no durability or profitability information, and which, as in the past, may prove impossible to maintain and thus sustain? ATI and APICA had previously implemented a lease/purchase program to help market palm oil presses; they decided to implement, on an experimental basis, a similar lease/purchase scheme for the maize mill, thus easing the risks associated with introducing a new technology.

MIDENO, which was created to target small farmers, was selected to implement the lease/purchase agreements. Its funds come from external sources: KFW, a German development bank, provides funds for coffee improvement credits, and the International Fund for Agricultural Development (IFAD) provides credit for the development of food crops. MIDENO grants credit to improve coffee production to underprivileged members of formal coffee cooperatives and it provides credit to develop food crops to members of both formal and informal groups. All MIDENO coffee and food production credits are provided as part of a planned development package that includes extension services, farmer supplies, marketing and other essential supporting services.

ATI provided MIDENO with the money to create a revolving loan fund to finance the lease/purchase of twenty mills by women's groups. MIDENO established two separate bank accounts, one for credit and one for lease payments, and a recording/accounting system for a lease/purchase fund. MIDENO also selected the women's groups who would receive the credit to lease/purchase the mills, signed the lease/purchase agreement with these women's groups and is responsible for all administrative procedures, including periodic collection of the lease payments.

MIDENO works closely with CATMI to enable the women's groups to lease/purchase the mill. Once the mill has been installed and the lease/purchase agreement signed, MIDENO disburses to CATMI an amount equal to the retail price of the mill. In effect, MIDENO has purchased the mill from CATMI; MIDENO owns the mill until the buyer has made the necessary payments.[18] Because a maintenance agreement with CATMI is included in the purchase price of the mills, its installation, the first two service calls and replacement of any parts under warranty are performed without charge by

CATMI. The women's groups are responsible for paying for any other necessary service, which is performed by locally trained repairmen. In theory, the women's groups are to call CATMI directly or call the local repairmen; in reality, because MIDENO credit agents usually are in the field, they tend to be the helper the women's groups contact first regarding any problems with the mill, and the agents relay the messages to the proper repair source.

The leases are paid in equal quarterly installments over a five-year period, following a grace period of only one quarter. The down payment required is 10 percent of the purchase price of CFA1,350,000. Lease payments include a finance charge equal to an annual interest rate of 10.25 percent. Of the 10.25 percent, MIDENO keeps half to cover the administrative costs associated with the lease/purchase arrangement.

A New Market?

Of the twenty-eight mills sold as of mid-1989, Anguh sold ten directly to private businessmen, who operate these as service mills. Eighteen mills have been sold to women's groups through the lease/purchase scheme with MIDENO.

MIDENO's recovery rate on all its loans for 1986-1987 was 94 percent.[19] MIDENO relies on FONADER's thirty-seven credit agents and six supervisors to receive and process lease/purchase applications and to collect the lease payments. Women's groups apply as a group; agents help them fill out the application. The groups are required to put up CFA135,000 (US$450) as a down payment to show their serious intent to set up a milling business.

The women's groups reported that the money for the down payments generally came from the sales of crops grown on communal—women's groups—farms. By May 1989, forty-four groups had submitted their applications to MIDENO; of these, eighteen had been selected to receive the mills under the lease/purchase plan. All eighteen mills had been installed by summer of 1989. MIDENO regulations stipulate that the mills must be located a certain distance from each other, depending on area population, in order to assure a viable market for the milling services.

Impact of the New Mills

The following is a summary of interviews conducted in July 1988, with women's groups who had been using the maize mill for at least three months. These impressions are included here to give the reader an idea of the impact of the mills.

Boyui, near Fundong

Membership. Thirty women comprise the group, which lives in an area where coffee is the major crop. Boyui, which originated as a social group in 1983, expanded to operate a large group farm; its major crop is corn. All members work the farm on weekends and when called upon during planting season. The group has its own bank account and controls its own earnings. In this area, however, the women said they turn individual earnings over to their husbands, after keeping some money for personal use.

The Maize Mill. Two years ago, this group identified a corn mill as a major priority. As soon as they learned of the availability of the lease/purchase plan they applied for a mill. They did not care about the model of the mill or about its costs, as they were sure they could repay the loan. To obtain the down payment, the women sold part of the corn raised on their communal farm and borrowed the remainder of the money from their husbands. The mill operates from 7 to 9 a.m. and 4 to 6 p.m., six days a week. Two men are employed part-time to operate the mill. The mill charges CFA50 per small bucket, a price set both to earn money and to serve the people. The mill serves seventy-two families; family size ranges from seven to ten persons. The money earned by the mill will be used first to pay off the loan and then to buy tools for the communal plot so that the women can grow more corn. The women would also like to buy a sewing machine to sew their own clothes and to build a combination meeting place/market where they would sell excess corn, beans and handicrafts. Before the mill was installed in April 1988, each woman would walk 3 km each way (forty-five minutes), five days a week to a maize mill in Fundam, where she paid CFA300 per tin.

Advantages of the Mill. The women interviewed cited the convenience of the mill, as well as its income-earning capacity. They say that when a visitor comes, *foo-foo* can be prepared in a short time. The time women spent walking back and forth to the mill can now be spent working in the fields or doing additional chores at homes. The villagers stated that they no longer have to fear for their children's safety. Previously, a busy mother might send her children to the corn mill, unaccompanied by any adult. The path to the mill crosses a major road (dirt track) and a stream. In winter of 1987, a child drowned crossing the stream. The group's conveniently located maize mill is within easy and safe access of all the villagers.

Baba I, of Ndop

Membership. Membership is composed of thirty-five Islamic women and one man, the vice president of the group. He serves as its spokesperson because the women speak only the local language.

History. Baba I was originally a social group; today the group owns a 5.5-hectare farm, where it grows corn, soybeans and vegetables. Proceeds from sale of farm crops are deposited in the group bank account. The group recently purchased a second income-generating asset, a cassava grinder.

The Maize Mill. The mill operates four to six hours a day, six days a week. The mill serves a large area (3–4 km radius) that provides a sufficient market for the milling and cassava-grinding services. Two men trained to operate both the mill and the cassava grinder are paid CFA6,000 per month each. At the time of the interviewer's visit, the operators were alternating work days because the cassava grinder was being repaired and the group had promised jobs to both men. Cassava and corn are the staples in this Muslim area. The group charges CFA50 for a small bucket and CFA150 for a large bucket. The women had compared various imported corn mills but purchased the Anguh mill because of the lease/purchase arrangement offered.

Advantages of the Mill. After all payments are made, the group plans to use the earnings to build a meeting hall/marketplace where they will sell the crops raised on their group farm. Prior to obtaining the corn mill in April 1989, the women would walk 3 km in each direction daily to privately owned mills or use individual handmills. Convenience was the major reason cited for having their own mill. Not having to walk one and a half hours a day each way to have their corn milled gave the women more time in which to grow more vegetables.

Of all the groups visited, this one was the most concerned about marketing. They did not want any more mills established within a 4 km radius; they realized the larger the area their mill served, the more money it would earn. They were aware of the location of every milling service within 10 km and the number of people each mill served.

Sumnyuy of Kibari

Membership. The group, whose name, Sumnyuy, means God's Farm, has fifty-eight members and is affiliated with a much larger, well-established women's cooperative. This group does not own or operate a communal farm. The mill is the group's first income-generating activity.

The Maize Mill. The Anguh maize mill is one of four in the area. The three others are imported mills; one is operated by one of the original "corn societies" founded by Elizabeth O'Kelly. Each mill serves fifty to seventy families in a specific neighborhood within a 2 km radius. The Sumnyuy mill charges CFA125 per tin; the mill owned by the corn society charges CFA100 per tin, as does one of the privately owned mills. Women in the area claim they always go to the nearest mill, as it would not be worth any women's time to walk an additional 2 km to save CFA25.

To obtain the money for the down payment, each woman was assessed CFA17,000. This fee presented no problem to any of the women, because they control the money that they earn from crops grown on their individual plots (corn, beans, ground nuts and potatoes).

Advantages of the Mill. Several women said that when their children had to go to the old mill 2–4 km away, they would lose a lot of corn on the way to the mill and flour on the way back. Now that the mill is nearby, these losses are substantially less. For the women themselves, not having to walk an additional 2–4 km each day means that they can spend more time farming and that dinner will be ready sooner. Young children can eat dinner and then go to bed, rather than having to be awakened for a late dinner. Although they live in an area where there are other mills, the women had not done any comparison shopping and did not care what type of mill they would be getting as "long as it could do the work" and they could qualify for the lease/purchase arrangement. Income earned by the milling service (after lease payments are made) will be used to purchase a cart or truck to transport corn from the field to their homes. Two operators for the mill share a salary of CFA5,000 per month.

Kong Mission Group of Santa

Membership. This group of forty-eight women was established seven years ago to "help each other to better ourselves." They maintain a group farm where they raise corn, Irish potatoes, leeks and other vegetables. They receive assistance from government agritechnicians and purchase fertilizer and other inputs as a group. In this area, *achu,* or taro, is the staple; corn is milled twice or at most four times per week.

The Maize Mill. The corn mill operates on demand, as the mill operator who is paid CFA5,000 per month lives on the premises. The mill is located in one room of a larger house built for this purpose and serves about 2,000 people (250 families). It charges CFA75 per medium bucket. The women officers said the mill is generating CFA20,000 per month and "they are very happy."

Previously, women had to go to the mill in Santa, 5–6 km by truck or one hour in each direction by foot. They say people think the quality of the flour ground by the Anguh maize mill is better (finer) than the flour ground by the mill in Santa. Therefore, if women from Santa know they will be traveling in the vicinity of the Kong Mission, they save their corn to bring to their mill. Because they were able to buy on credit, they did not compare the Anguh mill with any others.

Advantages of the Mill. Women claim that every compound in the area now is cooking *foo-foo* every day and thus people are eating better and getting a more varied diet (both corn and taro). Previously, because of lack of access to a corn mill and the fact that taro is the staple in this area, *foo-foo* was eaten only a few times a week. They are confident that more corn will begin to be cultivated in the area and women will earn more money by growing corn and selling it in the market. The group is seeking additional income-generating activities. Money earned is divided among the group members to be used for their individual needs—school fees, cloth and so forth.

Replication

ATI's innovative financial mechanism has inspired two other groups to start similar projects. Promotion of Adapted Farming Systems Based on Animal Traction (PAFSAT), an agricultural development project of technical cooperation between the Governments of the Federal Republic of Germany and Cameroon, recently made available funds, donated by a church group, to finance thirty corn mills by lease/purchase arrangements over a three-year period. PAFSAT's original plan was to use only imported mills in their project; now at least some of the thirty mills will be Anguh mills. PAFSAT Agricultural Program Advisor Klaus Zweier considers the corn mills an essential ingredient for further development. PAFSAT will be installing its mills in areas even more isolated than those in which ATI is working. He says, "Women spend countless time pounding the corn or else they have to walk as much as two hours with the corn on their head to get their daily food." IFAD will finance an additional ten CATMI maize mills in 1989 for sale (lease/purchase) to women's groups, and an additional, not yet determined, number in 1990–1993.

A Structured Market Strategy

If Anguh had just started to produce maize mills, he would have sold ten mills, not enough to break even, given all the design costs involved. By now he would have been bankrupt. The project identified a market niche for women's enterprises in rural areas. Through limited but much needed intervention by a number of NGOs and a government agency, two markets were opened for small and microenterprises. Anguh has been able to establish a solid production unit for the production of maize mills. As of June 1990, he was producing nearly one mill a week. This experience has led to the production of, among other items, palm oil presses.

The women's groups, too, have established small but significant income-earning enterprises. These groups generally reported earnings of CFA2,000/day, although some groups had data only for the past four months and their businesses were in the start-up phase.

In addition to the establishment of these enterprises, significant indirect benefits have accrued. All who were interviewed said that the time they saved by having their corn ground at a conveniently located mill allowed more time either to help their husbands with the cash crop, to work on the group farm, or to farm their own individual plots. In a village in a coffee-producing area, it was calculated that the additional labor women are now able to devote to their husbands' coffee crop should generate an additional US$127 per year per coffee farmer. Although not all the women could calculate the additional size of the land they would be able to cultivate, all of them expected their additional labor to result in more money.

Notes

1. Foreign Agricultural Service, U.S. Department of Agriculture figures are rough estimates based on reports of agricultural officers, trading companies and shipping records. USDA estimates are conservative compared with Food and Agricultural Organization (FAO) figures. No agricultural census is conducted in Cameroon.

2. John Madeley, "Cameroon Reaps Reward " (Washington, D.C.: *Development Forum,* May 1987).

3. International Labor Organization, *Technological Change, Basic Needs and the Conditions of Rural Women,* Report of the Joint ILO/Government of Norway Africa Regional Project (Geneva: ILO World Employment Program, 1984).

4. Marilyn Carr and R. Sandhu, "Women, Technology and Rural Productivity," UNIFEM Occasional Paper No. 6 (New York: United Nations Development Fund for Women, January 1988).

5. Edward Perry, Africa Project Officer, as reported in "Adapted Maize Mill Production in Cameroon," *ATI Bulletin* 12 November 1987.

6. Informal interviews conducted by Arleen Richman, 22–29 July 1988, with members of four women's groups that had purchased the maize mill and two groups that were operating other mills. Groups interviewed included Boyui near Fundong; Kong Mission Group in Santa; Baba I of Ndap; Sumnyuy of Kibari, near Jakiri (all owners of an Anguh/CATMI maize mill); and the members of the Jakiri Corn Society and the Jakiri Social Group.

7. Carr and Sandu, p. 52.

8. Elizabeth O'Kelly, *Rural Women: Their Integration in Development Programmes and How Simple Intermediate Technologies Can Help Them* (London: IT Publications, 1987).

9. Mark W. deLancey, "Women's Cooperatives in Cameroon: The Cooperative Experiences of the Northwest and Southwest Provinces," *African Studies Review* (March 1987).

10. Edward Perry, *ATI Project Plan,* Anguh Maize Mill, August 1985.

11. Survey conducted by Edward Perry as part of project plan preparation.

12. Perry, "Adapted Maize Mill Production in Cameroon."

13. Arleen Richman, informal interviews.

14. N. Nelson et al., "Foreign Area Studies for 1974," *Area Handbook for the United Republic of Cameroon,* p. 221.

15. Francois Tchakui, in formal interview with Arleen Richman in Bamenda, Cameroon, June, 1989.

16. Information in this section is condensed from a talk by A. N. Lantam on the "Types of Informal Groups in the North West Province and How They Are Being Used as Intermediaries for Rural Credit," 30 October, 1986.

17. Trip reports of consultant Carl Bielenbert (ATI records), August 1987.

18. For additional information on mechanisms of lease/purchase plans see Edward Perry, "A Key to Success: Institutional Infrastructure," *Macro Policies and Appropriate Technology Stimulate Small Enterprise Development,* ATI 1987 Annual Report, p. 32.

19. Statistical Information on Informal Groups (Bamenda: FONADER Agency, October 1986).

3 Introducing the Production of Appropriate Wheelchairs to Colombia

UNTIL SIX MONTHS AGO, LUIS ZUNIGA, aged twenty-five, had a good life. He lived with his parents and two brothers in a simple house in a lower middle-class suburb of Cali, Colombia. His father has been unemployed for some time; his mother works as a typist. One brother is in school; the other works as a bus-driver's helper. Luis had a job at a munitions factory. Although most of his earnings went to help his family buy necessities, with the money left over he was able to go with his friends to a movie or buy a beer at a local bar.

Then, on his way to work one day, Luis was hit by an automobile. Doctors have told him he will never regain the use of his legs.

After Luis was injured, his father went to several rehabilitation agencies, hospitals and commercial wheelchair stores to try to obtain a wheelchair. He found that imported wheelchairs were very expensive and that locally made chairs were also expensive or of very poor quality. His father learned that a re-habilitation center was offering purchasers credit to buy a high-quality, locally made chair, the Hotchkiss wheelchair. Although they did not have the money for the down payment, because credit was available Luis' family was able to buy him a wheelchair.

Luis now rides his wheelchair around the streets of Cali looking for an office job, because the munitions factory fired him when he could no longer work on the assembly line. Although he asked the company to give him an office job, it never responded. Luis says that being in a wheelchair makes it very difficult to find a job, even though he has a high school education.

Because there are many unemployed people in Cali, companies would prefer to hire them rather than a disabled person.

He is happy with his wheelchair and is thankful that he is still alive and able to move around. He says he is lucky he has a family who can take care of him. Although he does not have a job, he has resumed many of the activities that interested him in the past. His family is providing for his needs, he is mobile, and he is not a terrible burden on them. Luis is optimistic that ultimately he will find a job. He is reluctant to talk about the possibility that he will not—and that he will become an economic burden on aging parents.

Disabled people throughout the world are working to change the ways that they live, work and participate in their communities. Quality equipment that provides mobility is an essential element in their pursuit of independent, dignified living. People whose mobility needs cannot be met by crutches or canes need wheelchairs that will enable them to be as productive and independent as possible.

In the industrial world, wheelchair designers have responded to the increasing demands of disabled people by introducing lighter, faster wheelchairs, manufactured from space-age materials. Many special provisions—such as ramps and elevators—facilitate the lives of disabled people who are fortunate enough to live in developed nations. In the Third World, however, much less attention has been directed to these needs. Most of these countries have extremely limited resources; rather than focus on the needs of one special group, they have to be concerned about feeding their increasing populations and creating jobs.

In the United States, an estimated one person in 200[1] uses a wheelchair, and the numbers of wheelchair riders are estimated to be increasing. In developing countries, where available health care, including immunization against polio, is the exception and not the rule, the number of potential wheelchair users is at least in the same ratio, if not greater. Thus, in Colombia, with a population of thirty million people, we can estimate that there are 150,000 potential wheelchair users.

The typical potential wheelchair user in the Third World has been disabled by polio or a spinal cord injury and is unemployed or underemployed. If the person is employed at all, most likely he or she is self-employed. Although there are few reliable statistical data on the subject, begging appears to be the most common form of self-employment.

Obstacles to the Provision of Wheelchairs

Although a large demand for wheelchairs obviously exists in developing countries, any project to provide physically disabled people in these areas with wheelchairs needs to deal with four major obstacles: wheelchair design; local production of wheelchairs; financing to purchase wheelchairs; and marketing of the chairs.

Wheelchair Design

The first obstacle is that of wheelchair design. High-quality, state-of-the art imported wheelchairs are not designed for the rough conditions, such as muddy and rocky or uneven ground, unpaved streets and steps and hills commonly found in Third World countries. Third World wheelchair riders need chairs that can fold to fit through tiny doorways, chairs that occupy only minimal space in crowded living quarters and in the aisle of a bus. An ideal wheelchair in the Third World should be lightweight and easy to propel, yet it should be sturdy enough to withstand rough handling—such as being tossed on and off the roof of a bus. In traditional standard wheelchairs, the center of gravity is often far forward from the driving wheel; it is therefore difficult for the rider to self-propel the chair. It must not lose traction even when moving over rough ground. The wheelchair should be fully equipped with parking brakes for safe transfers, metal handrims for efficient propulsion and push handles for obtaining assistance.

Standard imported wheelchairs aren't designed to meet these requirements.[2] Imported wheelchairs in the Third World pose another problem: when the chair breaks down, the spare parts, such as the wire wheels and tires, and the skilled labor necessary to make the repairs often are not available.

Local Production of Wheelchairs

In several countries, standard wheelchair models are copied, and whenever possible locally available materials are substituted for their imported counterpart. The inferior materials used in the wheelchair's fabrication, coupled with an unsuitable design, result in a chair that does not provide true mobility to a handicapped person. Often, the low-cost wheelchairs are far heavier and more confining than the standard models; in addition, inferior materials do not withstand rough handling over a long period.

Financing to Purchase Wheelchairs

The third obstacle is financial. Because few wheelchair users in the Third World are employed, they cannot afford to purchase their own chairs. Most chairs are bought by family members or friends, or they are donated. In Colombia, as in many other countries, a wheelchair user can choose between a locally produced wheelchair that is moderately priced (US$180–$240) but of inferior quality, and an imported wheelchair. Prices for an imported wheelchair range from US$600–$1,500; the high prices reflect the limited supply. As the minimum monthly income in Colombia is 25,000 Colombian pesos (US$84), a poor or middle-income family cannot afford to buy an imported wheelchair for a family member or friend; without credit, they cannot afford a quality locally produced wheelchair either.[3]

Marketing of Wheelchairs

The fourth obstacle—marketing the wheelchairs—is related to the lack of finances. Many disabled people in Third World countries obtain their wheelchairs from rehabilitation centers; these wheelchairs are donated either by the government or by the private sector. Donors constitute an important market; the donors care about the numbers of wheelchairs they can distribute, but cannot evaluate their appropriateness. Disabled people who cannot afford to purchase a wheelchair are glad to have any chair; as passive beneficiaries of a rehabilitation center's largess, they do not complain.

When a quality product is marketed, the user should be viewed as someone who deserves the product. Disabled individuals in the Third World have little social status, both in their families and in their communities. Some cultures believe that a disability is a punishment for bad behavior in a previous life or a punishment inflicted by God. Disabled people are thought to be responsible, in some way, for their bad fate. This feeling contributes to the isolation suffered by the disabled person. How do you market a product that will be used by an isolated individual who has little status, little or no self-esteem and virtually no purchasing power?

Additional Obstacles to Wheelchair Production

Often, the family is ashamed of having a handicapped family member. Members try to keep the person hidden in their home and cut off any possible contact with the outside world. In other families, pity and love—rather than embarrassment—mandate that the disabled person be kept at home and not encouraged to live an independent life.

Whatever the underlying reason, most disabled people depend on their close relatives for all their needs—economic, social and emotional. This status prevents the disabled person from gaining any self-esteem. In addition, the disabled person exerts constant pressure on the family's budget. In a poor family, with limited resources, all hands must work to feed the family. In this sense, a disabled individual with no job has no value; instead of being an asset, he or she is a liability.

A high-quality, reasonably priced wheelchair built to withstand the rough conditions found in Third World countries could provide mobility to tens of thousands of potential wheelchair riders. Mobility increases their options and provides them more independence; they can leave the confines of their home and obtain an education and possibly a job.

There is another, often overlooked economic advantage to providing wheelchairs. Even if the disabled person cannot hold a job, being mobile generally relieves a potential wage-earner from having to stay home to look after the disabled family member. Mobility increases a person's self-confidence and can contribute to the entire family's overall sense of well-being and happiness.

The Project

The lack of supply of wheelchairs was especially serious in Nicaragua, where thousands of young people had become disabled in the Civil War. A grant of US$107,000 not only enabled the Organización de Revolucionarios Desabilitados (ORD) to repair existing models of wheelchairs but resulted in the manufacture of a new prototype wheelchair, suitable for local conditions. This wheelchair was designed by an ATI consultant, Ralf Hotchkiss, a mechanical engineer who has also been a wheelchair user since 1966. In addition to designing and testing the prototype, Hotchkiss, working with ORD, had the opportunity to experiment with tooling systems for its production. A second ATI project allowed him to refine and standardize the technology and test it in three regional training workshops in Latin America and the Caribbean.

Hotchkiss created a lightweight folding wheelchair that is well balanced, maneuverable, of simple but rugged construction and adaptable to an individual's body size and disability. Rear-wheel drive makes it easier to maneuver over rough surfaces. It weighs only two-thirds as much as standard chairs because of twenty-six fewer welds and eighty-two fewer fasteners.[4] The frame is made entirely of electrical conduit—inexpensive, sturdy tubing that is easy to shape. The chair can be folded to fit on the back of a donkey or the top of a bus. Standard automotive bearings and standard bicycle wheels are used; the seat is canvas. Several innovations in the Hotchkiss chair—including an improved braking system, armrest and footrest—represent significant advances in wheelchair design. Almost all production materials and components are available in most developing countries. Even more important, it can be manufactured at one-eight to one-fourth the cost of imported wheelchairs; its price is competitive with other locally produced folding wheelchairs that in most cases are inferior in design and quality.[5]

The Hotchkiss wheelchair has created widespread interest among wheelchair users who are self-employed and among rehabilitation workers. The almost unanimous reaction of the people questioned was that the Hotchkiss chair will significantly improve the users' mobility, especially over rough terrain.[6]

Training in Production of the Wheelchair

Between November 1983 and July 1986, ATI sponsored eight two-week wheelchair training workshops that provided forty-one participants with hands-on training in the technology of Hotchkiss wheelchair production. Ralf Hotchkiss organized and led the workshops, which were held in several countries in Central and South America. The participants, many of whom were wheelchair users, included mechanics from small businesses, vocational centers, social service agencies, and rehabilitation organizations. Some trainees had no experience in wheelchair production but all had some experience in light metal working and welding. During the workshops, each trainee built one wheelchair prototype to take home after the training. The chairs were constructed entirely of locally available materials with one exception: the front wheels had pneumatic tires. Participants in the training workshops came from Brazil, Colombia, Costa Rica, Dominican Republic, Guatemala, Guyana, Honduras, Jamaica, Malawi, Nicaragua, Paraguay, Peru, Sri Lanka, Trinidad and Zimbabwe.

ATI also sponsored a series of technical exchanges between Ralf Hotchkiss and wheelchair manufacturers in Latin America and Asia. The exchanges resulted in a number of improvements, both in local designs and in Hotchkiss' original prototype. For example, as a result of visits to a wheelchair factory in the Philippines, Hotchkiss incorporated the Tahanan curved armrest, which also serves as a fender, into the design; he also made suggestions that streamlined the wheelchair manufacturing process, reducing the weight of the chair by 25 percent and resulting in considerable cost and time savings for the factory.[7]

In November 1985, ATI published the manual *Independence Through Mobility: A Guide to the Manufacture of the ATI-Hotchkiss Wheelchair.* The manual includes illustrated step-by-step instructions for building the wheelchair: guidelines for starting a small manufacturing business to produce the chairs; detailed lists of tools, parts, and equipment; an explanation of jig-making techniques; and aspects of quality control and wheelchair maintenance. The manual is available in both Spanish and English.

The Hotchkiss wheelchair, which can be fabricated in small metalworking shops, has been replicated in ATI projects in Colombia, Peru, Guatemala, Honduras and the Dominican Republic. In addition, Hotchkiss wheelchairs are being produced by small enterprises in at least eight other countries—Brazil, Zimbabwe, the Philippines, India, Sri Lanka, Mexico, Paraguay and Bolivia— mostly by manufacturers who participated in ATI-sponsored wheelchair production workshops. This chapter will discuss only the Colombian wheelchair project. The Colombian project was the only one to receive three types of assistance—technical assistance to the production units, management and marketing assistance to the production units and financial assistance both to producers and consumers. Small businesses located close to major Colombian markets were to receive support to establish efficient and profitable enterprises and to create a national market for the wheelchairs. The purpose was to demonstrate the commercial viability and degree of market penetration that can be achieved, when the comparative disadvantages of microenterprises are overcome through institutional and collective action.[8]

The Colombian Project

Marketing Assistance

In the initial stages of the Colombian project, the implementing organization, Carvajal Foundation (FC), signed contracts with three existing metal workshops; most of these were already involved in wheelchair production. The producers were trained in the Hotchkiss technology, and quality was emphasized at all levels. For example, support for one potential producer was withdrawn early in the project when his shop failed to master the production technology.

Most of these enterprises were undercapitalized and needed additional capital to tool up to anticipated levels of production (planned production capacity was between 100 and 300 chairs per year) and to purchase materials and parts on advantageous terms. Technical assistance was provided to help the entrepreneurs choose tools, lay out their shops and institute quality control procedures. FC also helped organize joint sourcing of materials for the production units. Training in small business management practices was to be provided by the implementing organization or by local microenterprise support programs. The implementing organization was also responsible for marketing the chairs; the strategy would involve both the media—radio, television and newspapers—and the rehabilitation centers and hospitals. Finally, the implementing organization was to establish and administer a revolving credit fund that would be used to stimulate the sale and production of the Hotchkiss wheelchair.

Financial Assistance

According to the original project plan, each participating enterprise was to be offered loans for one, some or all of the following purposes:

- Credit-in-kind: acquisition of basic jigs and fixtures valued at US$1,000 each. During actual project implementation, ATI donated jig and fixture sets to each participating enterprise.
- Capital Assistance: US$2,000–$3,500 to purchase tools and other shop equipment; US$500–$1,000 for startup costs. In actuality, none of the Colombian enterprises received this type of assistance.
- Working Capital: US$2,000–$5,000, primarily to purchase materials and components. During project implementation, operation capital was provided in the form of advances. A producer would receive an advance equal to 50 percent of an order; this advance would be used to purchase the materials and components. The producer received full payment after the completed wheelchair passed the quality control inspection. Inventory costs were absorbed by the project.
- Sales Credit: A sales credit line was to be offered to institutional purchasers such as rehabilitation institutes and advocacy groups for the disabled so that these institutions could place large purchase orders and enter into rental/purchase agreements or extended payment (credit over time) sales with impoverished wheelchair riders. The sales credit component was designed to work as follows: An authorized institutional purchaser would place a large order (ten to forty chairs) with the organization administering the revolving loan fund (credit facilitator); the order would be placed with one of the participating enterprises. The purchaser would pay 6 percent cash prior to or at the time of delivery. The credit facilitator would loan the purchaser the remaining 94 percent; principal and interest were to be repaid quarterly over twelve to eighteen months. In turn, the institutional purchaser would sell the chair at its retail price; credit would be included in the retail sales and lease/sale contracts. Payments received on the retail sales contracts (principal and interest)

would mesh with the institutional purchaser's repayment schedule for the sales credit it received.

- Revolving Loan Fund: The various credit lines were to be incorporated into a single revolving loan fund; the fund's purpose was to stimulate production and sales of the Hotchkiss chairs. As the participating enterprises repaid their direct assistance loans and turned over their sales credit lines, the money made available would be used for additional sales credit to retail purchasers of the Hotchkiss chair.

The Implementing Organization

FC, based in Cali, was chosen to implement the wheelchair project in Colombia. FC is a private, nonprofit organization founded in 1961 to fund and promote programs that benefit the most economically depressed areas of Cali. FC's goal is to design models of community development that can be adopted by other institutions in other cities within Colombia and abroad. Its four major programs include a parochial centers program that encompasses education, health and recreation services; a low-income housing program that provides construction materials for low-income people to build their own homes; a microenterprise program that provides technical assistance, credit and management training to some 5,000 small entrepreneurs; and a similar program for shopkeepers or micromerchants.

As the implementing organization for the wheelchair project, FC was responsible for overall administration and financial management of the project; selecting the participating enterprises and subsequently providing managerial and technical assistance to subproject holders, including establishing quality control measures; establishing and administering a revolving credit fund; and promoting the Hotchkiss wheelchair.

Marketing Where There Are No Markets

The Everest and Jennings wheelchair, manufactured in the United States, is the best-known imported wheelchair, and until recently this company has dominated the world market. Because customs regulations in Colombia limit the importation of wheelchairs for commercial purposes, most of the imported wheelchairs in Colombia have been donated. Of course, donated chairs do find their way into retail shops, and some imported models are smuggled into the country. The government's policy does keep low-cost Taiwanese wheelchairs of older designs out of the Colombian market and in this way favors small-scale wheelchair producers.

Several producers in Colombia copy the Everest and Jennings wheelchair, using locally available materials such as wood and heavy metal. The largest manufacturer, located in Medellín, makes a low-quality, low-cost chair, marketed in the Bogotá-Medellín area. Its sales price of US$120 means it is afford-

able for a large number of consumers. It produces many chairs under government contracts for rehabilitation agencies. Better quality imitations of the
imported wheelchair are also available; they wholesale for between US$250
and US$350.

Competition in the wheelchair market in Cali is limited to two major manufacturers and several small work shops that only produce wheelchairs on special order. One of the major manufacturers in the Cali area, Klussman of
Palmira, fabricates the owner's own wheelchair model, an adaptation of the
Everest Jennings U.S. model, in addition to the Hotchkiss chair. Klussman has
been in the wheelchair business for thirty years; wheelchairs are his major
interest. Before contracting with FC, Klussman's shops used aged machines
that were mainly hand-driven but that had been built especially for wheelchair
production. The small workshops that manufacture wheelchairs on special
order, as a sideline to their regular business, rely on equipment used for other
metal-working activities; as a result, certain tasks such as bending the metal
cannot be executed as precisely as desired.

In late 1987, Rafael Diaz, a mechanical engineer, began producing high-quality Hotchkiss chairs in Bogotá. His workshop is a smaller operation than
Klussman's and produces only one type of wheelchair, the classic Hotchkiss
chair, which is sold for slightly less than Klussman's Hotchkiss chair.

Credit Availability

Klussman wanted to expand his wheelchair business, and he quickly realized
that the credit components of the project were far more attractive than other
available credit alternatives. Small enterprises can obtain loans in Colombia,
but the interest rates are high. For example, the Anglo Colombiana Bank
(ACB) offers personal, commercial and industrial loans for one year at an
annual interest rate of 36 percent. If the quarterly repayments are even one
day late, the interest rate becomes 48 percent. In addition:

- The lender must have an account with the bank for at least six months,
  with a positive average balance.
- Assets must be valued at 120 percent of the total amount of the loan.
- There must be a guarantor.

The small number of bank loans granted to small and microenterprises indicates the difficulties small businesses face in meeting the loan conditions.

In addition to commercial banks, credit may be obtained through two other
sources.

FC has a loan from the Inter American Development Bank (IADB) to be
used in its microenterprise program. IADB has set the following conditions for
the loan:[9]

- Sales maximum US$3,500
- Maximum value assets US$11,250

• Maximum family income US$630

FC is responsible for collecting data and screening loan applicants; it recommends worthy candidates for loans to The Foundation for Advanced Education (FES), which provides the loan. FES, a nonprofit financial institution authorized to operate both as a commercial bank and an investment bank, administers the IADB loan. FC recommends microenterprise program participants for two types of credit:

1. *Purchasing credit,* to be used only to purchase machinery and raw materials. The annual interest rate is 23 percent. If any payments are late, the enterprise has sixty days remaining to pay back the loan in full; then strict measures, such as foreclosures, are taken.
2. *Account credit,* to cover an enterprise's start-up costs. This loan carries an interest rate of 27 percent annually.

If a microenterprise does not borrow through FC's program, FES charges 36 percent interest annually; the amount of the loan cannot exceed ColP 1,000,000 (US$4,000).

Larger enterprises that do not meet the requirements of the IADB program can apply for loans to the Corporación Financieria Populár (CFP) or the Caja Sociál, both subsidized institutions established to extend social services and encourage small, fledgling enterprises.[10] There is no upper limit on the amount that can be borrowed, but there is a considerable waiting period until the loans are granted, during which time information on the applicant is gathered and processed. At least one guarantor is needed. Different interest rates are charged for different loans; the standard rate is 31 percent annually. Regular customers, who complete a management course and are recommended by FC, pay only 24 percent interest annually.

Consumers

Cali, Colombia, has a population of more than one and a half million people. A study conducted in July 1983 by the Corporación Regionál de Rehabilitación del Valle del Cauca (CRRV) (Cali is the center of the Cauca Valley) indicated that approximately 8,500 people in Cali were physically handicapped because of orthopedic problems or loss of a limb. The need for ambulatory devices such as wheelchairs ranked fourth among eight immediate concerns of families with disabled members. The study concluded that 63 percent of those people in the region who had some type of disability could be described as having limited resources. Projections estimated that in the year 1990 there would be more than 13,000 physically handicapped people in the Cauca Valley region.[11] Although no study was ever conducted for Bogotá, with a population of five million people no doubt there are more than 15,000 disabled people in this city and its immediate surroundings.

Marketing a product like a wheelchair presents a real challenge. Unlike the owner of, for example, a vegetable oil press, who will earn income by producing oil, the owner of a wheelchair will not necessarily earn income because of his or her purchase. Moreover, the product is expensive, and the need for the device is not backed up by purchasing power. And how does one locate the potential consumers? Most disabled people without a wheelchair spend most of their time at home, often hidden from society.

Disabled people do visit hospitals and rehabilitation centers, which traditionally have been the marketing channels to bring producers and potential consumers together. Cali has three rehabilitation centers that work with physically disabled people: CRRV, which works with physically handicapped people, alcoholics and drug addicts; Fundación Instituto de Ayuda Al Lisiado Julio H. Calonje, which works with people who are mentally retarded, are hearing impaired and who have physical disabilities; and the Fundación para Limitaciones Multiples (Foundation for Multiple Limitations), which works with mentally retarded people and people who are physically handicapped as a result of nerve disorders.

Hospitals and rehabilitation centers usually have some wheelchairs on site, but these are often old-fashioned models from the United States, which have been donated by charities. Because the rehabilitation centers are financially dependent on private and public contributions and donations, they do not have the money to buy large quantities of wheelchairs. Although they would be unable, on their own, to act as go-betweens for sale/placement of wheelchairs, rehabilitation centers and hospitals can provide information about the availability of the chairs.

Unfortunately, the people of the Third World generally do not trust official medical institutions. Many visit a doctor or a hospital when they have a serious illness or injury only to learn that there is no help or cure. Even if the doctor does prescribe a wheelchair, the rehabilitation center usually cannot provide one. Thus, not only are these people left without any help, they are also discouraged from seeking other medical help in the future.

Low-Income Families.   Most poor disabled people who own wheelchairs obtain them through charitable donations. For example, nineteen-year-old Rosa G. has been unable to walk since she was two years old. She lives with her mother and two brothers in a small house; her father deserted the family and her mother remains at home to take care of her. On her two brothers' combined income of ColP50,000 a month (approximately US$167) the family could not afford any type of wheelchair. Because Rosa was too heavy to carry around, she was forced to spend most of her days in bed. One day, two years ago, Rosa's mother carried her to the front of the house so that she could enjoy the sun. A woman walking by was so touched by Rosa's situation that she bought her a wheelchair. Using her wheelchair, Rosa, escorted by her mother, now is able to leave her house and enjoy some mobility.

Organized charities often assist these families. Father Gallo has a widely listened-to radio show carried on Radio Caracol. On one program, which dealt with the needs of disabled people, he asked the Cali community to donate money for wheelchairs. The contributions received financed the purchase of five chairs, which were given to poor, disabled people. Although this type of appeal did bring results, it was not a systematic way to provide mobility to large numbers of disabled people.

Middle-Income Families. Families who earn a moderate income usually buy a locally produced, low-quality wheelchair. These families realize that a high-quality wheelchair is beneficial, but they must buy a wheelchair they can afford. Usually every family member works outside the home; having a wheelchair makes it possible for the disabled person to remain at home alone. Using the wheelchair, the disabled person can move around the house and take care of his or her own needs. Depending on age and goals, some disabled people use their wheelchairs to go to school or to try to find a job so they can become more independent.

Technology[12]

The Hotchkiss production system was developed so that a small metalworking shop can produce the chair locally. Welding, bending and routine mechanical skills are the principal labor skills required. Batch processing of components precedes the final assembly of chairs. Economies of scale are reached with an output of as few as two chairs a week. The production technology is labor intensive; approximately forty hours of work are required to produce a chair.

The primary unifying element in the production system is the set of special tools developed by Hotchkiss. A set of dies and a bending frame ensure the uniform size of the components, and a set of jigs ensures that welding angles and placement of components are correct and uniform. Uniform tooling combined with the procedures illustrated in the production manual ensures that the integrity of the design is maintained in numerous and isolated workplaces.

Technical assistance emphasizes quality control procedures. Quality-enhancing production procedures include pre-stressing wheel spokes and heat strengthening frames after welding, two procedures used by quality-conscious bicycle manufacturers. Because a batch system is used to fabricate components, it is economical to subject all components to a detailed inspection prior to assembly. All chairs are put to a hard-use test prior to sale. If at least one wheelchair user is employed in the workshop, the chairs can be tested at zero opportunity cost. The production manual emphasizes quality control procedures as a major element in the production system.

Periodic inspection of the wheelchairs is conducted by qualified representatives of the local implementing organization, who apply inspection standards developed by the technical contractor. Producers who meet standards are entitled to use a seal of quality backed by the local implementing organization and ATI. The ultimate goal is to have inspection procedures controlled by an association of users.

The frame of the current Hotchkiss model is made entirely of electrical conduit—cheap, sturdy tubing that is easy to shape. The unique swing-away footrest and curved armrest are also made from this material. The chair folds with a simple tubular frame made from half the usual number or parts. Standard automotive bearings and standard bicycle wheels are used; the seat is canvas. Several of Hotchkiss's innovations, including his improved braking system, and the armrest and footrest, represent significant advances in wheelchair design. These already have been copied and incorporated into design work in the United States. One of the most original developments is the footrest, which allows maneuvering in tight spaces and close access for difficult transfers. Another unique feature of Hotchkiss's chair is the armrest. A curved fender bar has replaced a removable armrest that was bulky, expensive and difficult to construct. Because the bar follows the shape of the tire, the armrest does not hinder transfer into the chair.

In designing each of these new features, Hotchkiss had to consider carefully the kinds of tools, techniques and materials required in the manufacturing process. Each change was evaluated in terms of simplicity, cost, availability of materials and the necessary production time.

Between September 1986 and November 1988, 381 Hotchkiss wheelchairs had been sold in Colombia. Most of these were marketed through the Consumer Credit Fund administered by the CRRV. CRRV, a nonprofit organization founded in 1961, the Year of the Handicapped, promotes, assesses, directs and supports programs that benefit those members of the community who are physically and/or mentally limited. CRRV has an established network among Colombian social service agencies and organizations working with disabled people; in the Cauca Valley alone it is affiliated with some forty rehabilitation institutes and social service agencies. CRRV is located in the center of Cali and is very visible. Approximately 95 percent of the funds CRRV receives come from the private sector. Because CRRV is financially dependent on gifts, it is difficult for it to make consistent projections of income for future years.

The CRRV Credit Plan

In addition to marketing the wheelchair, CRRV now administers the revolving loan fund. It processes the loan applications, collects the repayments and submits quarterly progress and financial reports detailing the status of the credit fund to FC. In September 1988, under an agreement executed between CRRV and FC, CRRV assumed full responsibility for managing all project funds, including the producer and consumer credit components. Carvajal Foundation transferred all project assets to CRRV and its involvement in the project ended as originally planned.

CRRV charges an annual interest rate of 26 percent on loans given to people who purchase the Hotchkiss wheelchair. Only purchasers of Hotchkiss wheelchairs are eligible for loans. CRRV claims that most loans are repaid on time at CRRV headquarters. Through June 1988, only 11 percent of the payments were late, and only 1 percent of the loans were in default. If payments are not made on time, the interest rate is increased to 38 percent annually, and CRRV sends an employee to locate the purchaser and collect the money.

The loans provided by the ATI-funded project are for a maximum of 24 months with an average 20 percent down payment required. Repayment schedules are structured according to family income. Five basic payment plans are offered by the program. Five percent of the total 26 percent interest pays CRRV's administrative costs. Until May 1987, the retail price of the wheelchair was the same as the manufacturer's selling price. At that time, the retail sales price was increased to offset administrative costs (the price in May 1988 was ColP55,000 = US$186). CRRV claims that this increase, coupled with the interest payments, falls short of covering the administrative costs. In June 1988, when the authors visited Colombia, CRRV voiced its concern about this problem. FC would no longer be acting as a risk buffer by purchasing the wheelchairs, and CRRV was preparing to assume responsibility for the credit fund.

In analyzing these circumstances, it is apparent that the revolving credit fund is running the risk of decapitalization. To maintain the purchasing power of the total credit fund, the interest rate needs to reflect the inflation rate, the rate of nonpayment and the administrative costs. If the credit fund is to remain viable, a balance must be reached between an increase in interest rates and an increase in sales price.

The retail sales price must be within the range of middle-income consumers. If the sales price is too expensive, purchasers will buy a less expensive model elsewhere. A higher-priced chair also places an additional burden on the family members who must make the monthly payments. Relaxing the credit terms to allow repayment of the loan over a longer period of time may solve this problem, but too long a repayment period may negatively affect the fund. In September 1989, CRRV restructured its credit terms; loans now are granted for a maximum of eighteen months (rather than twenty-four months), although most loans are for twelve months. The interest rate remained at 26 percent, and 20 percent down payment of the purchase price is required.

Special Marketing Strategies

CRRV, together with FC, has designed a specialized marketing strategy to reach the identified target group, disabled poor people. Their strategy views the wheelchair user as someone with specific needs.

CRRV took advantage of FC's access to a newspaper and radio station in Cali and its own links with most of the nation's social service agencies to launch an aggressive marketing and advertising campaign. Ads in the telephone book's business pages, in the newspaper and over the radio compared the Hotchkiss wheelchair to other available models and stressed its practical and social benefits. Ads and brochures also publicized the availability of credit to wheelchair customers.

The radio was found to be the best medium to reach the target group. Most disabled people who do not own a wheelchair spend their days in bed, listening to the radio. Almost everyone, even the very poor, owns a radio. Advertisements were broadcast over three popular programs, "Pase la Tarde con Caracol," "Summy" and "Paco Luna." Advertisements also were placed in the Friday, Saturday and Sunday editions of the Cali newspaper, *El Pais.*

Brochures were distributed to rehabilitation centers and hospitals in the Cali area to be given to interested individuals. The hospitals were ideal information channels because they had been able to observe the wheelchairs' performance for some time. When the project first began, the Hospital Departmental had purchased eighty wheelchairs; Hospital Beneficencia del Valle had bought eight chairs.

When it realized that marketing efforts were not reaching the poor, CRRV initiated a campaign to locate sponsors for needy consumers. Groups such as the Catholic Church identify low-income potential wheelchair users from needy families. The sponsor, usually a well-established local business, makes the down payment and pays 50 percent of the monthly installment; the family pays the remainder—approximately US$100—through the consumer credit fund.

Local Workshop Programs

Currently, two workshops are making high-quality Hotchkiss chairs in Colombia, one in Cali and one in Bogotá. As part of the project implementation, Carvajal Foundation signed contracts with three small enterprises (two in Cali, one in Bogotá) that appeared to be capable of and interested in producing the Hotchkiss wheelchair. These producers received tool kits and were trained in the Hotchkiss technology. Experience indicates that prestart-up technical training is essential to successful wheelchair production. They also received FC's microenterprise training, which provided the management skills and support they needed during the risky startup phase.

In Cali, the two entrepreneurs who initially undertook production of the Hotchkiss wheelchairs were Klussman and Rodrigo Hernandez. Hernandez had been making hospital beds, fences and other metal products and was much less experienced than Klussman. Hernandez, who had been trained by Hotchkiss in Costa Rica, envisioned the wheelchairs as a side activity until it became profitable enough to be engaged in full-time. Hernandez no longer is producing wheelchairs. After he produced a few chairs that did not meet the quality standards set by FC, FC withdrew its support for his enterprise. Hernandez claims he did not find wheelchair production profitable enough to justify his concentrating on only this activity.

Klussman is convinced that making wheelchairs is a profitable business. To date he has produced approximately 350 Hotchkiss wheelchairs. After FC selected him as a subcontractor in 1984, he was trained by Hotchkiss in Lima, Peru. Klussman has concentrated on producing only one product—wheelchairs—and is dedicated to his product. The only major problem he encountered was the lack of twenty-four inch wheels, a result of the country's import restrictions. He solved the problem by modifying the wheelchair design to accommodate the readily available twenty-six-inch wheel. All the other raw materials are available locally. Two of his employees are wheelchair users; not only can they test the chairs on site but they also can answer questions likely to be asked by the ultimate users.

The original Hotchkiss wheelchair is sometimes called a semi-sports model. Its curved armrest and maneuverability make it ideal for active young people who have full control over their upper bodies. Older people nearly always prefer a hospital-type model, outfitted with special adjustments. A hospital model looks like the typical imported wheelchair commonly seen in hospitals, airports and medical supply stores. The padded removable armrests and height provide less mobility but more comfort and support. Because older people represent the largest share of the market in Colombia, the market for hospital chairs is greater for it than for the semi-sports design.

For these reasons, Klussman began manufacturing two models of the Hotchkiss chair: the classic Hotchkiss design that is the semi-sports model and the hospital version, which has padded armrests and flat foot rests. In March 1989, the semi-sports model sold for about US$192 and the hospital version sold for US$212. The hospital model with foldable footrests that are standard on the semi-sports model can be purchased for US$206. Klussman provides a full one-year guarantee at no cost to the wheelchair user. Moreover, he offers (at a minimum cost) adaptations for special-purpose wheelchairs, such as headrests and seat belts.

In June 1988, Klussman was selling 50 percent of his production of Hotchkiss wheelchairs to FC to be marketed through CRRV. Ten percent were being exported to Panama, and 3 percent were exported to the United States. The rest were sold directly to hospitals. Klussman credits the project with making all this possible. The training and technical assistance he received gave him the technical knowledge to produce a better quality of wheelchair. Because FC was willing to buy the wheelchairs he produced, he was able to take the risk involved in upgrading his production. This was important when he first entered the project and began the process of switching from producing low-quality wheelchairs to high-quality chairs.

At present, helped by a loan from the Corporación Financieria Populár, he is completing the final stage of machine modernization. This is expected to increase his workshop's production capacity to 100 wheelchairs per month. Seventy percent of his production is his own version of a hospital chair, which he sells for US$207, slightly less than the Hotchkiss model hospital chair he also produced. Thirty percent of his production is devoted to his two versions of the Hotchkiss chair.

The Bogotá Enterprise

The Bogotá entrepreneur, Rafaél Diaz, is producing thirty Hotchkiss wheelchairs per month. His enterprise, COLEQUIP, Ltd., produces a slightly less expensive version of the classic Hotchkiss design, this is the only wheelchair he fabricates. Eighty percent of his production is sold directly to rehabilitation agencies; 20 percent is sold through CRRV's consumer credit fund.

Diaz, a mechanical engineer who has access to metalworking machines, was trained by Ralf Hotchkiss in Berkeley, California in June 1986. In late 1987 he received an advance from FC to purchase raw materials to produce his first batch of chairs, which were completed in early 1988. He has obtained additional advances from FC and a loan from Projuventud. Diaz employs three people in his wheelchair business, which shares facilities with his other initial business—chicken feeders.

The Purchasers: A Sample

Availability of consumer credit has been the key to the success of the wheelchair project.

Only purchasers of Hotchkiss wheelchairs are eligible for loans, and this is the only credit currently available to purchase a wheelchair in Colombia. As already noted, the purchasing power of the end user is extremely limited. The decision to purchase a wheelchair is usually made by family members, who are responsible for the disabled person's well-being. In Cali, the majority of the families who purchased wheelchairs had a total household income above the minimum wage set by the Colombian government. Many disabled people who already owned a wheelchair found out about the Hotchkiss model and asked if this wheelchair could be purchased for them when their model broke. Most of these disabled people owned low-quality, locally produced wheelchairs that did not provide them enough mobility to live independently and, in particular, to hold down a job. Interviews with Hotchkiss wheelchair riders who were selected to participate in the qualifying rounds of the ABILYMPIC Games for Handicapped People in Medellín, revealed that this was the first time most of them had actually taken a trip unaccompanied by their parents.

Another sample of ten people living in Cali who owned a Hotchkiss wheelchair were interviewed. Five of these were older people who had become disabled as a result of an illness such as arthritis. They lived with their children, who took care of them. Using the Hotchkiss wheelchair, they were able to get around the house and go to the hospital or rehabilitation center. None of these older people expressed a desire to have a social life outside their homes, although they found it hard to accept the fact that they were no longer as mobile as before their illnesses. Because most of their families were of the middle class, they did not need to earn any income.

Four of the ten wheelchair riders were young; two girls, age seven and nineteen, were both physically and mentally handicapped. Because they are totally dependent upon their parents, the wheelchair did not provide them the opportunity to take charge of their own lives. The wheelchair did make it easier for their parents to move them around. The other two young people had been students when they became disabled. They planned to re-enter school once they gained skill in using the chairs. These two youths were shy and a bit scared about the thought of leaving their homes.

Luis Zuniga's experience is typical of the difficulties faced by wheelchair riders, especially in developing countries. When the project was conceived, the idea was that credit would be provided not to families, but directly to disabled people, contingent on a business' commitment to employ the disabled person, who then would be able to repay the loan out of earnings.

FC may start to ask that large companies offer employment to disabled people instead of or in addition to sponsoring 50 percent of the cost of the chair for needy consumers. It is difficult to convince companies to employ disabled people in an already oversaturated labor market.

Most of the people who were interviewed said that credit availability was the major reason why their families purchased the Hotchkiss wheelchair. For some of them it was the only way they could afford a wheelchair. Quality was less important. Some people did note, however, that the reputation for quality and an affordable price prompted their decision to buy the Hotchkiss chair.

In conclusion, this project can be described as successful. It does, however, point out how difficult it is to market products to the very poor. There is an additional obstacle in this case—the fact that the end users have limited mobility. Disabled people have to put forth special efforts to gain access to independent living and are hampered not only by their lack of mobility, but by economic and social barriers. In Colombia, inroads are being made to market the chair to poor people, but it will clearly take considerably more time than was anticipated.

A preface to a 1984 paper on the Hotchkiss wheelchair reads:

> Providing mobility to handicapped persons living in the Third World is the obvious goal of the Hotchkiss Wheelchair project. Two additional concepts embodied in the project design—providing employment opportunities and credit facilities for the handicapped—testify to ATI's holistic approach to appropriate technology. The wheelchair was designed so that handicapped persons can participate in all aspects of the production process: from blueprint modification, to welding, to fabricating the final product. ATI now is encouraging the local project partners to experiment with employment practices that enable the workers to repay the credit extended to buy their own wheelchairs. Thus, the Hotchkiss wheelchair project not only will free many Third World residents from the confines of their homes, but will also increase their self confidence and self-esteem, and will contribute to their overall sense of well-being and happiness.

Klussman's wheelchair manufacturing enterprise in Palmira does employ two wheelchair riders. Though only a modest step toward the holistic approach described above, it nonetheless may hint that the broader dream will yet be realized.

Notes

1. *Project Plan: Regional Wheelchair Production,* (Washington, D.C.: Appropriate Technology International, 1984), p. 3.

2. John Guy Smith et al., *Wheelchairs for the Third World* (Washington, D.C.: Appropriate Technology International, 1984), p. 1.

3. Exchange rate ColP299 = US$1. *International Financial Statistics* 42(10) (1989).

4. Project Plan, p. 8; *Wheelchairs for the Third World,* p. 4.

5. Richard Chavis, *Market Analysis of Wheelchairs in Colombia* (Washington, D.C.: Appropriate Technology International, 1988), p. 3 (mimeograph); *Wheelchairs for the Third World,* p. 1.

6. Project Plan, p. 4.

7. *Wheelchairs for the Third World,* p. 4.

8. Project Plan, p. 20.

9. Information provided by Maria Mercedes Holguin, Director, Microenterprise Program, Carvajal Foundation.

10. Information provided by Nancy Dominguez Moreno, Coordinator, Wheelchair Project, Carvajal Foundation.

11. Richard Chavis, *Market Analysis,* pp. 1–2.

12. Ralf Hotchkiss, *Independence Through Mobility: A Guide to the Manufacture of the ATI-Hotchkiss Wheelchair* (Washington, D.C.: Appropriate Technology International Project Plan ATI, 1984); pp. 9–10; *Wheelchairs for the Third World,* pp. 6–9.

4 Introducing the Production of Glazed Pottery in Rural Villages in Tanzania

NDUGU IRIOKO E. M. KITURURU, a Tanzanian, has been interested in pottery for many years. Kitururu dreamed about owning his own small pottery workshop, where he would make beautiful items and teach pottery crafts to others. He was convinced that there was a demand for quality ceramic products in the rural areas of Tanzania and that his business would be a success.

A few years ago he resigned his teaching job to devote all his time and energy to learning the pottery and ceramics business. First, he went to India to study the Indian wheel and Indian pottery techniques; subsequently, he was awarded a one-year scholarship by a Tanzanian parastatal to study pottery in Japan.

When he returned to Tanzania from Japan, he moved to Same, a village near the highway to Dar es Salaam. He rented a workshop close to the Kilimanjaro Industrial Development Center (KIDC) factory and a small shop in town where he could sell his products. The manager of KIDC permitted him to use the KIDC kiln without charge and gave him all the technical assistance he required. He experimented with glazed kitchenware, and people came from many miles around to buy his products.

Then a new manager was appointed at KIDC. When this manager was faced with a directive that KIDC—and all parastatals—cover its operating cost, he stopped providing technical assistance and kiln use to Kitururu and other local potters, whom he viewed as competitors. If Kitururu were to make glazed ceramic ware, he would have to build his own updraft kiln.

Searching for a loan to finance the kiln, Kitururu traveled throughout Tanzania, without success. When he learned that the Centre for Agricultural Mechanization and Rural Technology (CAMARTEC) had received funds from Appropriate Technology International (ATI) to finance village potteries, he applied for a loan, but received no response.

Without a kiln, Kitururu was unable to produce any pottery, had to give up his small shop, and was forced to live off his savings. Then he built a simple kiln, which cannot fire glazed ware but is adequate for the traditional fired products, like flower pots. Today, he still produces only unglazed ware, and CAMARTEC has not processed his loan. Recently, with money obtained from a family member, he began building an updraft kiln. When this kiln is completed and he has had time to produce a considerable amount of ceramic ware, Kitururu plans to hold an exposition in Moshi, the nearest city. He hopes that this will re-establish his reputation as a potter. Although he still believes that he will have a successful business, he has become frustrated and bitter.

Unglazed tableware produced by rural potters in Tanzania faces increasing competition from imported plastic and aluminum kitchen and tableware. The rural potters lack both the technology and the capital to enter the market for glazed ceramics, an upgraded product that should be in demand at the village level. This chapter describes an effort to transform rural potteries in Tanzania into a commercially viable, economically sustainable industrial sector.

The Political Context: Rural Industry for Local Self-Reliance

Tanzania has just begun to explore its enormous deposits of local clays, the primary raw material used in the pottery industry. As more geological investigations are carried out, most of the other minerals used in making the glaze are expected to be discovered. Until now, these minerals have had to be imported and purchased with scarce foreign exchange.

Few other industries are as profoundly traditional as pottery. Pottery is one of the oldest industries or, more correctly, crafts, known to man. It is encouraging that in Tanzania, as in many other developing countries, hand-fashioned pottery has survived the introduction of modern, capital-intensive mass production technologies.

The production of quality terra cotta ware entails little more than a wheel and an updraft, high-temperature kiln. Both are relatively affordable by rural villagers. Thus, potteries are a natural rural-based industry that uses locally available raw materials and produces for both rural and urban markets.

Development of the pottery industry closely corresponds to the rural development goals of the Tanzanian government as outlined in the Arusha Declaration of 1967, which enunciated the principles of socialism and self-reliance. In the Arusha declaration, President Julius Nyerere described the type of communal cooperation his government sought to foster. The declaration asked the government to consolidate its control over the means of production, prepare development plans that did not depend on foreign assistance and place greater emphasis on improving rural living standards.

These goals were to be achieved by mobilizing domestic resources, reorganizing the rural areas into concentrated settlements (*Ujamaa*) and increasing state control over industry, trade, insurance and banking activities. Campaigns to resettle rural people in the so-called *Ujamaa* and development villages were carried out from 1969 to 1976.[1]

Twenty years later, development experts hold mixed views on the success of this program. Major progress has been made in raising education and health standards. Tanzania's literacy rate of 60–80 percent is one of the highest in Africa. In addition, an extensive network of health centers is located throughout the country.

On the other hand, Nyerere's resettlement program had a singularly negative effect on agricultural production. Moving peasants into villages located 1.5–2 miles from their land placed additional burdens on their already difficult existence. The establishment of villages also disrupted traditional farming systems and the previously stable relationship between animal husbandry and agriculture. Village-based farmers could no longer maintain as many animals as they did when living on their farmlands. In addition, the decision of newly established communities to assign lands near village centers to agriculture and outlying areas to grazing reduced soil fertility and other benefits of traditional tenure and land management systems. Because farm tenure in Tanzania is leaseheld, "villagization" led to an unwillingness to invest in land improvements, such as measures to prevent soil erosion.

Villagization has been only one of many factors contributing to declines both in Tanzania's economic growth and in the day-to-day existence of the Tanzanian farmer. Other important factors include oil price increases, the fall in world market prices for coffee and sisal, the collapse of the East African community, a war with Uganda and drought.

Since 1985, the Tanzanian government, under Ali Hassan Mwinyi, has taken notice of the domestic factors influencing allocation of scarce resources and has implemented economic policies that emphasize agriculture. The National Economic Survival Program, Tanzania's fourth five-year plan and the Structural Adjustment Program stress the need for agricultural growth. Adjustments included a 40 percent devaluation of the Tanzanian shilling (TSh) against the U.S. dollar in June 1984, revisions in land tenure and land use, improvement of agricultural marketing, promotion of agricultural cooperatives and reductions in both recurrent and development expenditures. The immediate effect of these changes, however, has been to worsen living conditions of the ordinary Tanzanian citizen. Civil service salaries have been reduced and the legal minimum wage of TSh1,500 per month (US$15)[2] is inadequate to provide for even a small family of two children (GNP per capita US$250).[3]

Inflation (officially 30 percent, unofficially 50–100 percent), devaluation of the Tanzanian shilling and the decline in domestic agricultural production have led to both price increases and food shortages. Many shops carried only a few products, carefully interspersed between flowers to fill the openings on shelves. Thus, the need for ordinary Tanzanians to generate additional income is greater today than it was twenty years ago, at the time of the Arusha declaration. In this respect, the pottery industry can make a modest contribution.

Traditional Pottery Production

Traditionally, pottery has been produced seasonally, by women in their spare time. Making and selling pottery supplements either farm income or salaried employment. In rural villages, earthenware consists almost exclusively of cooking pots and water jars. The manufacture of these items entails virtually no production costs. Clay is available locally, and cow dung or wood to fuel the pit can be collected easily. The only equipment needed is a stone for smoothing, a curved stick and skilled hands. The average potter may produce approximately 100 to 150 pots each year, which she can then sell at local village markets. Interviews with these women potters reveal that apart from their labor to prepare the clay, collect cow dung for fuel and mold the pots, the only nonlabor costs are those they incur in transporting their products to nearby rural markets.[4] The median price of pots is about TSh300; the actual price depends on size. With transport costs averaging about TSh20 per pot, additional income per household can range from TSh28,000 to TSh42,000 annually (US$280–$420). In rural areas, where cooking takes place on traditional clay stoves, the marketing of terra cotta ware has proved not to be a problem. In the cities, however, where modern stoves are more prevalent, clay cooking pots represent only a small part of the total market for kitchenware.

Village-Owned Potteries

Village potteries are owned by both men and women. They use more advanced technology and employ full-time trained workers (most often men) to produce low-fire unglazed ware. There are approximately twenty-five village potteries throughout Tanzania. These potteries use pottery wheels and a permanent kiln that necessitates a higher capital investment than does artisan production. The need to purchase firewood also increases production costs. The market for the ware produced by village potters is small, uncertain and mainly in urban centers where pots serve decorative purposes. Without local markets to absorb their production, the long-term future of these village potteries is uncertain. One way to expand market opportunities would be to introduce glazes that would make ceramic ware waterproof, attractive and more durable.

As a rule, village potteries are labor intensive. Potters collect their own clay and prepare it by mixing, filtering and adding soft minerals, such as shale. The clay is then thrown on a kickwheel, flywheel or the original Indian wheel. Kilns are constructed of locally produced red building bricks, which cannot withstand the 1,100°–1,200° C temperature needed for glazing.

Although women are almost always the traditional potters, village-level potteries appear to employ only men. Women fashion pots from clay by hand at home; once a wheel is introduced and the worksite is moved away from the home, men take over the job. Even the Women's Association, which operates a pottery in Singisi, as discussed later, employs only men in the pottery. The location of the worksite has important implications for male/female distribution of labor. It is still too soon to determine how the gender issues affected this project. The authors suspect that if several of the village potters had been female, they might have responded more quickly to the opportunity presented by the project.

The Pottery Industry

In addition to artisan and village potteries, ceramics are also produced on an industrial scale. Currently, three industrial enterprises in Northern Tanzania produce glazed pottery: the KIDC, a parastatal organization funded and operated by the Tanzanian government and the Japan International Cooperation Agency (JICA); Bujora Pottery, a production-cum-training center in Mwanza; and Sherif Dewji and Sons, Ltd., a private firm in Arusha. Although the three companies are not identical, a description of one of them gives a good indication of the state-of-the-art of the technology used in the Tanzanian industrial ceramics sector.

Sherif Dewji and Sons, Ltd., is managed by Ali Sherif, who oversees the operations of the company's five main divisions (woodworking, cement block production, pottery production, production of bonemeal and storage facilities). Each of the divisions operates independently. The company is housed in a series of godowns (storage facilities) formerly used for the seed and coffee bean trade. His primary interest, however, is pottery production, the largest and oldest division, which occupies two godown bays—an area of about 30,000 sq. ft.

Sherif Dewji and Sons decided to engage in pottery production some twelve years ago when it realized that the Tanzanian economy would be able to support only those activities based on local materials and manufacturing techniques, not those based on imports. Once the decision had been made to shift from trade to small-scale industry, two family members traveled to India to study local pottery production. Experimental work began in 1977, and in 1980 the company allocated two large godown sheds to expand pottery production. Since then, efforts have focused primarily on consolidating operations. A permanent installation includes heavy duty equipment such as ball mills, filter presses and mixing tanks. Production has also graduated from sole dependency on hand throwing to mechanical production in motor-driven devices (machines), which ultimately might replace hand throwing altogether.

Initially, the company imported its glazes from abroad, but after Tanzania's war with Uganda in 1979, shortages of foreign exchange made further imports impossible. Fortunately, after a period of trial and error, Sherif Dewji and Sons was able to identify local substitutes for most of the minerals used in imported glazes. Sherif, however, had little success in producing firebricks from local materials. It was not until 1986 that it, with the help of Appropriate Technology International (ATI), was able to produce a reliable, well-formed and durable firebrick. The company continues to improve the tensile and insulating characteristics of the brick by adding ball clay and sawdust to the material mix and testing different pressing techniques.

Growing Demand for Pottery Products

In 1977, a market survey carried out by the National Development Corporation revealed considerable demand in Tanzania for all types of ceramic products.[5] National demand for tableware was estimated at 1,250,000 mugs, 350,000 plates and 50,000 bowls per annum. Assuming an average production of 45,770 mugs, 12,900 plates or 1,875 bowls per village pottery, current domestic demand for ceramic ware (calculated at 1977 demand level plus 5 percent growth per year) would be sufficient to support at least forty-nine such potteries (see Table 4-1).

The figures in Table 4-1 may significantly underestimate actual demand, as increased energy and transport prices and the devaluation of the Tanzanian shilling have made alternative products of plastic and aluminum increasingly expensive and scarce. By producing durable glazed ceramic ware that can be competitive in price with plastic and aluminum, village potteries have a new window of opportunity.

Table 4-1   Demand for Crockery: Potential Number of Village Potteries

Items	Total Demand, 1977	Calculated Demand, 1988[a]	Average Annual Production/Unit
Mugs	1,250,000	2,244,820	45,770
Plates	350,000	628,550	12,900
Bowls	50,000	89,793	1,875

[a] 1977 demand + 5% growth per annum.
Source: Constructed by authors based on data from a market survey by the National Development Corporation, published in Ndugu James Tomecko, "Alternative Strategies for Developing Pottery in Tanzania" (Arusha: Small-Scale Industries Development Corporation, 1977).

Obstacles to Producing and Marketing Glazed Pottery Ware in Tanzania

The Tanzanian ceramic market is comprised of three separate markets. The traditional market is typically supplied by local women potters who produce cooking pots and water jars. The intermediate market is supplied by village potteries that produce vases, ashtrays, flowerpots and tableware. The industrial sector in Northern Tanzania produces industrial ceramics such as insulators and electric outlets, as well as tableware and other items for domestic use.

Shortages in the domestic supply of foreign exchange have reduced the availability of aluminum and plastic products, which in turn has created an excellent opportunity for village potteries to sell glazed pottery at the village level. To do so, however, these potteries must upgrade their kilns and gain access to both firebricks and locally produced glazes. Until 1987, neither of these products existed in Tanzania. Even if these products had existed, potters would not have had access to the capital needed to purchase them.

Market Forces: Transport

Any analysis of markets and marketing in Tanzania must deal with the issue of transport, for it is transport that links producers and consumers in this nation of more than 22 million people. Transporting fragile ceramic ware is especially problematic in a country such as Tanzania. Good roads are scarce, and secondary roads are often impassable during the rainy season. There are few vehicles of any kind, let alone trucks equipped to haul large quantities of fragile pottery. Purchasing a vehicle requires foreign exchange, which is limited. Gas is expensive: Its price of TSh40 per gallon as of August 1989 sharply increased because of the crisis in the Persian Gulf that started in August 1990. Maintenance costs are also phenomenally high.

Most people travel in public transportation (buses) or private cars that pick up fee-paying passengers; neither of these vehicles can accommodate large quantities of pottery material. Although the lack of transport has hindered expansion of local market opportunities, it has also effectively protected village-based potteries from the dumping of glazed pottery by the national ceramic industry.

The Competition

Traditional Pottery

The traditional market consists largely of unglazed cooking pots and water jars. Plastic containers increasingly replace water jars, but earthenware jars do keep water cooler. Aluminum or iron pots have made few inroads in replacing the traditional terra cotta cooking pot. Not only do traditional pots supposedly improve the taste of food, but the curved terra cotta pot and the stove on which it is placed form an integrated unit. Together, they have a relatively high energy efficiency compared to either aluminum or iron pots used on the same stoves. Before aluminum or iron pots can become popular, therefore, a major change in cooking methods must take place. For these reasons, rural villages in Tanzania still provide a stable market for traditional pottery, produced by village women. Because the pots are sold in village markets located near the actual place of production, traditional pottery has an important advantage over other products that must be transported from the cities.

The Ceramic Industry

The three big ceramic industries in Northern Tanzania produce glazed table-ware, industrial products such as insulators and electrical supplies and decorative pottery such as vases, flowerpots and ashtrays. They tend to target city markets, but occasionally they dump some products at nearby village markets.

Because they are partly or fully mechanized, the industries produce in large quantities and can maintain high quality standards. As established businesses, they have access to formal credit channels and are therefore able to respond quickly to the changing demands of the market.

The ceramic industry's major competition comes from the plastics and aluminum industry. To maintain its market share, the ceramic industry has had to improve the quality of its ceramic tableware, yet maintain competitive prices.

As a result of Tanzania's recent foreign exchange crisis, plastic and aluminum products have become more expensive. In addition, because transport costs have also increased, many traders have stopped carrying the low-profit plastic and aluminum ware to make room for more profitable items. The resulting limited availability of plastics and aluminum ware increases the demand for ceramic products.

Although village potteries and large-scale ceramics producers should be producing for different market niches, at least one of the large ceramic companies, KIDC, now views the village potteries partly as potential competitors. Until recently, KIDC's primary focus was the transfer of production technology to rural areas, rather than commercial success. KIDC trained local rural potters in the entire process of ceramic manufacture, from raw material preparation to decoration. A scholarship program permitted outstanding local potters to study for one year in Japan.

Although assistance to rural potters continues to be part of its mission, KIDC has turned into an aggressive commercial producer of ceramic tableware and a strong competitor. The KIDC plant produces 2.5 metric tons of tableware per month, which is sold mostly to the Tanzanian Tourist Corporation. All revenues go to the Tanzanian government. The former manager of KIDC, who stopped providing technical assistance and kiln use to local potters, embittered at least one village potter, as illustrated by the story of E. M. Kitururu at the beginning of this chapter. The management has since changed.

The New Customers: Village Potteries

The focus of this study is the small village potteries that produce manually crafted, unglazed cups, vases, ashtrays and flowerpots. Production is small, artisan and, contrary to current market forces, directed to the urban market, where two challenges must be overcome. The first is the abundance of imported plastics and aluminum ware. Although this situation is likely to change because the lack of foreign exchange needed to purchase the plastics and aluminum, the scarcity of tableware will probably surface first in the villages. The second, given the production concentration on kitchenware, is the stiff competition from the large ceramic industries, which are urban based and therefore have easier access to the city markets.

Strategically, the logical market for kitchen and tableware would be the villages themselves. As plastic and aluminum ware become scarce, the ceramic producer who is nearest the market would enjoy a comparative advantage.

For village potteries to survive, they must fill this market niche. To do so they need access to technology that will enable them to produce durable, good quality glazed pottery at a competitive price. The technology is available in Tanzania. Some of the large ceramic producers are eager to teach village potters glazing techniques because this will create new markets for their own glazing materials. To produce glazed pottery, village potteries must also upgrade their kilns. Traditionally, village pottery kilns are built of red clay brick that can withstand firing temperatures of no more than 800° C and melt at a temperature of 1000° C. For glazed pottery, firing temperatures of at least 1100°–1200° C (1300°–1400° C for local glazes) are required. To build such kilns requires special firebricks, which, thanks to the assistance provided by Sherif Dewji and Sons, are now produced from locally available materials.

Availability of Investment Capital for Village Potteries

To improve their kilns and adopt the technologies required to compete in local markets, village potteries need access to financial resources. Do village potters have access to money-lending institutions? What options are open in theory? What is available in fact? When the Tanzanian government realized how important small-scale industries were to domestic economic growth, it began to set up programs to assist them. Initially, two national banks, the Cooperative and Rural Development Bank (CRDB) and the National Bank of Commerce (NBC) were responsible for providing financial resources to small-scale industries.

Cooperative and Rural Development Bank

The CRDB was established in 1971 as the state-owned Tanzania Rural Development Bank. Since 1984, ownership of the bank has been divided between the government (which holds 51 percent of its shares) and the Cooperative Union Tanzania, which was created to assist small-scale industries to purchase equipment. The CRDB makes both traditional loans and provides lease/purchase arrangements to small-scale industries in the areas of agriculture, oil extraction, weaving and spinning, carpentry, welding, fruit canning and manufacturing.

Although, in theory, any small industry with fewer than fifteen employees can apply for a loan, the authors of this chapter found no record that any village pottery ever applied for a loan to expand operations.

The CRDB insists that a potential investment be commercially viable and that the owner be experienced in running a business. To ensure this, they visit the business, look at the record books if they exist and collect information through their nearest branch office. Inasmuch as most small industries do not have the elaborate information required readily available, gathering such material nearly always takes considerable time. Banks are aware of this problem, yet they have not modified their information requirements. It is hardly surprising that of the six hundred loan applications the bank received in 1987 to purchase a maize mill, only twenty loans were awarded.

The CRDB sets a number of conditions for loans:

- The amount loaned can be no more than 67 percent of the total investment. They prefer a 50/50 division.
- The grace period is three years at 21 percent annual interest rate.
- Collateral, preferably in the form of immovable assets is required. If no immovable assets are available, insurable movable assets not older than three to five years are sometimes accepted.

National Bank of Commerce

Originally established as a commercial state bank, the NBC was persuaded by the government in 1984 to begin financing small-scale industries. The NBC evaluates financial assistance applications on the basis of the project's viability and current national priorities for social and economic development in the industrial sector. In the case of small-scale industries, the bank will finance up to 85 percent of the total investment; for medium- and large-scale industries, the bank will finance as much as 75 percent. Normally the bank will consider individual loan applications only for a minimum of TSh100,000.

The conditions for a loan follow:

- The maximum grace period is three years with a repayment period of ten years, which includes the three-year grace period. The interest charged is 27.5 percent annually.
- When appropriate, the NBC may require potential borrowers to offer security in the form of mortgages, or third party guarantees adequate to cover repayment of the principal. This is not routine, however, and collateral often can be enough. For immovable assets or property, a title (Offer of Right of Occupancy) deed or ownership certificate is requested.
- Information is required about the project, its assets, the clients, its location and so forth. Theoretically, a feasibility study is also required, although in practice loans have been processed without one.

As is the case throughout Africa, many parts of Tanzania still operate as a subsistence economy. In such areas, the implications and potential of money as an unrestricted universal medium of exchange are not fully understood. This lack of understanding, the banks argue, is one reason why requests for financial assistance have increased slowly. The banks have responded to this problem by implementing programs to educate the public and by expanding promotional communications. Every Thursday the NBC places advertisements in the local newspaper; its representatives go into the field to explain what services they have to offer, and they promote their activities through word of mouth.

Those who have tried to obtain loans tell a dramatically different story. They mention the bureaucratic delays, a problem in most state institutions. Small businesses often need immediate cash to respond quickly to changes in demand. If the entrepreneurs have to wait too long, they might be forced out of business.

The authors found two other reasons why there are relatively few loan applications. Banks, especially the NBC, have little experience in dealing with small enterprises. They treat them the same as they do large industries and require them to provide information that is not readily available and that may be irrelevant to small-scale operations. In addition, there is the embarrassment factor. Many villagers are fearful of being unable to repay a loan.[6]

Removing the Obstacles

Organizing the Project

Two organizations have been involved in upgrading village potteries: CAMARTEC and Sherif Dewji and Sons. CAMARTEC was formed in 1984 as an amalgamation of Tanzanian Agricultural Machinery Project (TAMTU) and the Arusha Appropriate Technology Project (AATP). It is a national parastatal institute, with headquarters in Arusha. Under its new mandate, CAMARTEC seeks to test technologies applicable to the rural sector, and to promote the production and sale of useful hardware. It also manufactures a limited range of agricultural equipment such as ox-carts, twinshare plows and planters. Historically, it has concentrated on farm-related technologies, but it is now involved in water storage and pumping, solar power, bio-gas and local manufacture of consumer durables. Under its present parliamentary mandate, it is empowered to enter into cooperative agreements with international organizations and to administer donor funds.

CAMARTEC's involvement in the project takes place at two levels. First, it monitors the project and manages the project funds, most of which were provided to Sherif Dewji and Sons, as a five-year interest-bearing loan. These funds, once repaid, are to be used for new project activities jointly agreed upon by ATI and CAMARTEC. Second, CAMARTEC helps small potteries, when appropriate, to complete loan applications to SIDO (Small Industry Development Organization) to obtain capital.

Sherif Dewji and Sons provides training, firebricks and glazes. After they train potters to produce glazed pottery, they sell them the firebricks for the kiln and glazing materials. CAMARTEC arranged a loan to Sherif Dewji, which the firm used to purchase these materials in bulk.

Producing Firebricks and Glazing Material Locally

After a few delays, Sherif Dewji and Sons started to produce firebricks. Although the first bricks were brittle and cracked easily, subsequent small adjustments in the mixture and firing methods have permitted a steady production of good quality firebricks. The development of new underdraft kiln designs was instrumental in enabling Sherif to achieve firing temperatures of 1300° C and higher. Improvements were also made in the oil firing mechanism of the kiln.

Glaze material can now be produced locally. The glaze is of good quality, although the required firing temperatures are still high. Sherif Dewji and Sons, at its own expense, is experimenting further to substitute imported minerals with locally available material, in order to reduce costs as well as to permit lower firing temperatures. Potters from Mwanza and other districts who were not included in the project have come to Sherif Dewji for information on the different kinds of glazes as well as to purchase the glazing material and firebricks.

Entering the Market

This study was completed in 1989, three years after the project began. In spite of the availability of firebricks and glazing material, few of the targeted fifteen village potteries have begun producing glazed ware to any significant degree. Two potteries have upgraded their kilns and begun to shift their production line from flowerpots, ashtrays and candles to tableware, but glazed tableware is not the major focus of their production. For example, one pottery in the village of Singisi now produces a monthly average of twenty unglazed vases, forty unglazed flowerpots, one hundred cups (fifty glazed) and a number of other items. Total monthly sales average between TSh15,000 and 20,000 (US$150–$200), with operating expenses of about TSh8,000 (US$80), but glazed ware is fired only once each month. The Singisi pottery continues to focus on flowerpots, vases and some *jikos* (charcoal stoves). A pottery established two years ago in Moshi still is experimenting with glazes; it produces fewer glazed items than does Singisi.

Why have the village potteries been so slow to upgrade their operations? Lack of available financing is one obvious bottleneck. The president of the Women's Association in Singisi, which operates the pottery there, believes that insufficient credit is available to purchase enough glazing materials to produce an ample supply of glazed tableware. She claims that she needed to have, in stock, a sufficient inventory of glazed ware to be able to assure the customers that the tableware they want to buy will be available at all times.

If village potteries are to produce for rural markets, they must have sufficient financing to offset the slower rate of inventory turnover; items in rural areas can remain on the shelves for some time. Lack of financing mandates that the village potters sell their ceramic ware quickly, to generate enough money to purchase materials for their next batch. To reach a large number of potential buyers, the village potteries aim for the urban markets. Cash flow problems explain why potters elect to sell batch production to a larger store in the city, at a lower price, rather than to hold out for a higher price in the villages. On the other hand, if potters do not market their products in rural areas, rural demand will not be created.

Interviews with village pottery centers in Arusha and Kilimanjaro districts reveal that most potteries still concentrate on reaching the big urban market. Is this decision to produce for the urban market based on lack of financing, inadequate cash flow, lack of knowledge of the rural market and the potential therein or the status associated with the city?

The potters themselves identify the improved technology with upgraded urban rather than rural markets. To use the words of the potter Kitururu: "I want to wait until I have produced enough glazed items to organize a big exposition in Moshi to establish my name and maybe even a shop." In order to build a special kiln for firing glazed materials, he had stopped producing unglazed items and subsequently had to close his little shop in the center of Same, his village. Whether he succeeded in penetrating the urban market was not known at the time this book went to press.

The Ceramic Industry and Village Potteries

The distinctive market niches for the village potteries and the ceramic industry have not yet fully materialized. Although Sherif Dewji & Sons has withdrawn from the production of tableware, both in rural areas and in towns, the larger KIDC sees the village potteries as potential competition.

Sherif believes that the tableware market should be the domain of village potteries; he says that increased transport costs prevent and will continue to prevent the ceramic industry from competing successfully in rural areas. Therefore, at present Sherif Dewji is concentrating on producing firebricks, glazing materials and industrial ceramic products such as electric insulators and electric wall outlets—articles that are easier to mass produce than tableware.

Availability of Innovative Financing Schemes

Manufacturing glazed tableware is still risky for most rural producers. The quality demanded by an urban market is difficult to maintain, and transport costs are high. These place rural potteries at a disadvantage in competing with ceramic industries operating in the urban areas. Initially, the urban market appears to be attractive, partly for psychological reasons, partly for pragmatic business reasons. Because lack of financing forces the village potters to turn over their inventory as rapidly as possible, they seek a market where there is a large concentration of customers. This market is the cities, the area where rural producers encounter competition from the ceramic industries.

CAMARTEC has not performed well as a financial intermediary. Though several small loan applications were eventually submitted to them, no funds were ever disbursed. In retrospect, one can question whether CAMARTEC was a good choice for handling such matters. It was, after all, a research and development organization, not a financial intermediary.

In addition, CAMARTEC is a parastatal institute laden with the bureaucratic hurdles inherent in virtually all government agencies and local banks. That this situation has persisted for three years, however, is unfortunate. It has undoubtedly discouraged many potters who at one time might have been interested in the project and might be willing to take risks. The fact remains, however, that without adequate financial resources and some risk sharing, it will be almost impossible for a small village pottery to make the switch to glazed pottery.

Local Initiative

One of the most important, yet unforeseen, results of the ATI-funded ceramics project was the establishment of the Tanzanian Ceramic Association (TCA) in May 1986. The initial participants in the first TCA workshops were the project in Singisi, the Sherif Dewji Pottery Works in Arusha, the Ceramic Institute in Mbeya and the Sukuma Museum in Bujora. Any pottery workshop in the country is eligible to become a member of the association, regardless of its size, production capacity or number of employees. Currently, there are nine member organizations from the northern zone and nine from the south. The aim of the association is to bring together under one institution both established and fledgling pottery workshops throughout Tanzania. The goals of the TCA are as follows:[7]

- to encourage the use of modern pottery techniques through sponsorship of seminars and practical training sessions in Tanzania and abroad;
- to ensure a free exchange of ideas and experiences among various pottery workshops in the country by publishing regular newsletters and holding annual meetings;
- to promote the identification and use of locally available ceramic raw materials, and to seek assistance to import those materials for which local substitutes cannot be found;
- to encourage local fabrication of simple pottery machinery and equipment;
- to educate the public and secure markets for ceramic ware manufactured by Ceramic Association members through exhibition and publication of articles in newspapers, and other media; and
- to establish closer relations with government and parastatal institutions engaged in research and in promotion of small-scale industry.

Between 1986 and 1988, the Tanzanian Ceramic Association sponsored five seminars. The earlier seminars sought to focus attention on the importance of potteries in general, but later meetings have emphasized more technical aspects of pottery production. A seminar in June 1988 focused on opportunities for financing and strategies for small enterprise management. Handouts showed examples of cash flows and emphasized the importance of maintaining accurate business records. A representative of CAMARTEC spoke about the possibilities for soft loan schemes for small potteries.

The TCA has the potential to become the instrument that will provide rural potteries with raw materials, inspire ideas and help them secure small loans. This is what ATI hoped Sherif Dewji and CAMARTEC would have achieved under the project.

Conclusions

Assessing the design of the project, one might conclude that the technical assistance component of the project's objectives was achieved. But a number of questions still have to be answered about the market and the competition. As it is known that glazed tableware costs only a fraction more than plastic and aluminum ware, why have the potteries not switched the bulk of their production from unglazed ware to glazed ware? Is there any market for glazed ware in the villages?

It is difficult to separate the issue of lack of financing from the issue of defining the market. The market behavior of those potteries that made the transition and are selling their ceramic ware in bulk in urban areas indicates that lack of financing is the overriding concern.

Thus far, the original assumptions regarding the growing demand for pottery products and the fact that upgraded potteries can penetrate the village market have not been proved. There is reason, however, to remain optimistic. Although the village potters have not yet moved into the rural market, the potential is there. In fact, when Sherif Dewji significantly reduced production of glazed tableware, the potential market for village potteries substantially increased.

To sell their products successfully, village potters may need training in marketing (and becoming aware of changing market conditions). Although the project did not provide this training, the TCA has identified the need for market training as essential to the success of village potteries.

In retrospect, one has to question the choice of CAMARTEC as the financial intermediary. CAMARTEC's staff clearly did not have the expertise to process financial applications and necessary training was not provided. Because the local banking system does not function well, the role CAMARTEC was to play is still very much needed. Recently, the TCA began administering a revolving loan fund, established with project funds. The TCA, too, lacks expertise in this area. It has one advantage, however, that might prove the key to success. Members of the TCA are motivated and they have the incentive to perform this function well. The entire pottery industry, be it the large ceramics companies or the village potteries, will all benefit if the TCA program becomes successful.

Notes

1. A. B. Herrick et al., eds., *Tanzania: A Country Study* (Washington, D.C.: American University, 1978), pp. 89–90; and ATI Project Plan No. 840103, 1984.

2. Exchange rate, August 1988: TSh99 = US$2.00 *International Financial Statistics*, 42(10) (October 1989).

3. *World Bank* Report (Oxford: Oxford University Press, 1988).

4. According to interviews with women in Singisi, they were producing only for the rural markets, although Singisi is close to Arusha. It may be that selling prices are a little higher here than in more remote areas.

5. Ndugu James Tomecko, "Alternative Strategies for Developing Pottery in Tanzania," speech at SIDO seminar held 14–16 April, 1977, Arusha. Mimeograph by SIDO Regional Office, Arusha.

6. This is not limited to small-scale enterprises. Sherif applied for a loan with the NBC and could meet all the requirements. He waited for six months and, when the bank still had not responded, he withdrew the application.

7. Tanzanian Ceramic Association, paper distributed by establishment in 1986, Arusha, p. 9.

5 Introducing the Production of Improved *Jikos* in Kenya

RACHEL GUMBA, her husband and their seven children live in a modest home on the outskirts of Nairobi. Her husband works as a clerk in a government office. Although she took a secretarial course in school, she has not been employed since her second child was born. The Gumba family cooks on a *jiko*, or charcoal stove—as do more than 80 percent of the families in Nairobi.

In April 1987, Rachel saw an improved *jiko* exhibited at a fair. She was told that cooking on the improved *jiko* would save a lot of money in charcoal costs, as it was considerably more energy efficient. She was convinced and purchased the improved *jiko* for the special offering price of 60 Kenyan shillings (KSh).

Two years later, Rachel agrees that the improved *jiko* really has saved money in charcoal costs. For example, she says that when she was using the traditional *jiko*, she used to buy two sacks of charcoal each month to cook meals for her family. Now she buys only one sack of charcoal each month, a savings of KSh90 per month. Mrs. Gumba was the first in her neighborhood to own an improved *jiko*; most of the other women have followed her example.

This chapter was based on the research by Eric Hyman and Stijntje Schreurs in association with Ton de Wilde. Material in the chapter draws heavily on papers by Dr. Hyman: "The Strategy of Production and Distribution of Improved Charcoal Stoves in Kenya," *World Development* 15(3) (1987), pp. 375–386; "The Economics of Improved Charcoal Stoves in Kenya," *Energy Policy* (April 1986), pp. 149–158.

One and a half years later, she was still using the same improved *jiko*. Although the liner had to be replaced once, it was not difficult to locate a replacement liner and an artisan to install it.

Although the improved *jiko* clearly has paid for itself in savings on charcoal costs, Mrs. Gumba is most enthusiastic about its greater safety. She explains that "with seven children, and a crowded house, several children usually are in the kitchen area. Earlier, with the traditional *jiko*, the metal became very hot and several children were burned—fortunately, not badly. The improved *jiko* is much safer because the ceramic liner insulates the heat much better."

Jiko is the Swahili word for a small stove used extensively in Kenya. There are two major types of *jikos*—some are designed to burn wood; others burn charcoal. In rural areas, households usually own a woodburning *jiko* because wood can be gathered without charge. Urban households, which have to purchase either wood or charcoal, prefer charcoal-burning *jikos* because charcoal takes up less space, is ready to use without chopping and burns more evenly.

In 1985, 17 percent of rural households and 83 percent of urban households in Kenya owned charcoal-burning *jikos*. Although charcoal may be as expensive per unit of heat generated as kerosene, liquefied petroleum gas or electricity, a charcoal stove is much cheaper than stoves for these other fuels because it does not have many imported components. In some areas, the supply of charcoal, which is made from wood, is more reliable than the supply of fossil fuels.

The majority of low-income urban dwellers live in small quarters where space is at a premium. A charcoal-burning portable stove takes up little space and can be used with a variety of traditional or modern cooking pots. In addition, in upland areas, where nighttime temperatures can drop below freezing, *jikos* are used as space heaters.

Wood Scarcity and Charcoal Consumption in Kenya

Real incomes in Kenya have been declining recently, while the population growth rate has risen above 4.25 percent per year (1984). Thus, Kenyans are becoming increasingly dependent on locally available energy sources. Charcoal consumption is expected to increase more than 6.5 percent per year between 1988 and the year 2000, assuming there are no changes in government policies or in the type of stoves used.[1]

The sustainable supply of wood in Kenya for all purposes is estimated to be 13 million tons per year. In 1985, the demand was 18.3 million tons, including nonhousehold uses, leaving a net shortfall of 5.3 million tons per year that was filled by depleting the stock of trees. These stock depletions are unevenly distributed across the country. Table 5-1 shows how the percentage of current forest stocks is expected to decline by the year 2000 if existing trends continue. An average of 8.33 tons of wood is needed to produce 1 ton of charcoal in traditional earth pits or mound kilns. In 1984, Kenyans burned 775,000 tons of charcoal, which required the consumption of 6.45 million tons of wood.[2]

Table 5-1   Cumulative Forest Stock Depletions Expected by Area in the Year 2000 (in percentages)

Central/ Nairobi	Coast	Eastern	North Eastern	Nyanza	Rift Valley	Western
33	24	19	0	52	29	36

Source: O'Keefe, Raskin and Bernow, "Energy and Development in Kenya: Opportunities and Constraints," in *Project Plan Ceramic-Lined Jikos* (Washington, D.C.: Appropriate Technology International, 1985).

The projected annual consumption of charcoal by Kenyan households in the year 2000 is 2.1 million tons. The predicted mean annual increment of wood for the year 2000 would meet only 35 percent of the total demand for wood and charcoal fuels. This shortfall would lead to unsustainable tree-cutting rates and decreases in wood stock, but it could be reduced if households adopted more fuel-efficient charcoal stoves.[3]

As the consequences of deforestation have become more visible, nature and the environment have become topics of serious discussion in Kenya. Because charcoal is only 50 percent as efficient in net energy delivery as firewood, research has been ongoing in Kenya since 1977 to improve the efficiency of charcoal stoves.

The Consumers

Charcoal is a costly necessity for most poor urban households. For example, in Nairobi, charcoal purchases consume 20 to 25 percent of the budget of a laborer's household.[4] The price of charcoal varies by season, location and volume of purchase. Transport costs vary with distance from the source of the charcoal. The official price of charcoal in various locations is set by the Ministry of Finance. The schedule of prices has not changed since late 1982, but the price controls are not rigorously enforced.

Charcoal is scarcest during the rainy season when wood is harder to collect. The weather interferes with charcoal production in outdoor earth pits or mounds and agricultural labor requirements are at their peak. Charcoal makers produce more charcoal during the dry season because they need more cash. It is also easier to transport and store charcoal during the dry season. Because price controls do not permit seasonal price fluctuations, during the rainy season sellers reduce the weight of charcoal packaged in sacks.

Retailers buy charcoal in sacks from wholesalers. A sack contains about 30 kg of charcoal. Another 2–3 kg of charcoal dust, twigs and sometimes stones are sometimes deliberately added to the sack. During the dry season, 1 kg of charcoal purchased by the sack costs an average of KSh2–2.5 in Nairobi and KSh1.5 in other areas. During the rainy season, charcoal costs an additional KSh1 per kg.

Many households cannot afford to buy a sack at a time; others are afraid that a sack of charcoal will be stolen. Consequently, most households buy charcoal in small tins, or *debes*. Although sold by volume, these units usually weigh 1–4 kg. No effective controls exist on the retail price of charcoal in tins. Purchased by the tin, charcoal costs an average of KSh3 per kg in Nairobi and KSh2 per kg in other areas.[5]

Charcoal costs an average user of a traditional *jiko* in Nairobi KSh166,[6] where KSh700–800 (US$41–47)[7] is an average laborer's income.[8] The average charcoal user in other urban areas, where charcoal prices are lower, spends KSh110. Those rural households that use charcoal consume a smaller quantity of charcoal and pay a lower price than do the urban dwellers. A rural user may spend KSh68 per month for charcoal, but this amount could be an even larger share of household income than that in Nairobi because rural incomes are lower.

Traditional Jikos

The traditional *jiko* was introduced in Kenya near the turn of the century by Indian workers and artisans recruited to help construct the railway. This *jiko* became the standard cooking stove for the urban poor and the middle class. It is shaped like a cylinder and has a door for draft control and ash removal. Three legs support the round base, and three hinged, triangular-shaped flaps hold a single cooking pot. The unit has a metal grate and a handle. Because the traditional *jiko* is not insulated, it radiates heat out to the air as well as to the pot. The most common size is 29 cm in diameter and 28 cm in height, including the legs, and weighs 3 kg. The basic design has changed little since it was introduced ninety years ago.

Production

Traditional *jikos* are made almost exclusively in the informal sector by small groups of two or three artisans. On average, the artisans spend about one-third of their time making *jikos;* the rest of the time they produce other items such as buckets and cooking dishes. [9]

Only a few basic tools are needed to make a traditional *jiko*: a chisel, an anvil (usually made from a short length of railway track), a punch and a hammer. Scrap sheet metal (usually old oil or chemical drums), rivets and a round bar are the only required raw materials. These cost an average of KSh20 per stove. The basic forms of the *jiko* are chiseled out from the metal and joined to the base. Sometimes, templates are used. Firebox doors, legs and potholder supports are attached by riveting. The traditional *jiko* sells for KSh30.

A skilled artisan can make as many as seven traditional *jikos* a day. Although a full-time *jiko* maker could earn KSh70 per day (net), an artisan usually manufactures *jikos* only in response to the demand.

Table 5-2 Price, Expected Lifetime and Efficiency of Stoves Used in Kenya

	Traditional Jiko	Bell-Bottom Stove	Umeme Stove	Haraka[a] Stove
Retail price in Nairobi (KSh)[a]	30	65–85	85[b]	70
Parts needing replacement	Metal grate	Ceramic liner/ grate and insulation	Metal grate	Metal grate
Price of replacement parts in Nairobi (KSh)	10	30[c]	15–20	20
Frequency of replacement of parts (months)	3	8–12	6–12	6–12
Expected lifetime at full use (months)	12	24	48	24
Efficiency in laboratory tests(%)[d]	20–22	29–32	33–36	28–31

Sources: Steve Joseph, Yvonne Shanahan and Peter Young (1982) Bill Stewart (1984); Hugh Allen (1985); N. Claassen (1985); Maxwell Kinyanjui (1985); Heinz Schneiders and Jules Mkallata (1985); in Eric Hyman, "The Strategy of Production and Distribution of Improved Charcoal Stoves in Kenya," *Energy Policy* World Development 15(3) (1987): p. 378.
a Conversion rate: US$1 = KSh16
b The artisans receive scrap metal through UNICEF at a reduced price. At market prices for scrap metal, the Umeme stove might cost KSh120 and the Haraka stove might cost KSh100.
c Including labor.
d PHU^2 (percentage of heat per 2-liter unit) is the percent of charcoal's heat used in boiling and evaporating 2.0 liters of water for 60 minutes.

Efficiency

The thermal efficiency of the traditional *jiko* is relatively low. The percentage of heat used as measured in a laboratory in bringing water to boil and simmering for sixty minutes is approximately 20 percent.[10] Controlled cooking tests in the field show an even lower efficiency of 18 percent.[11] Because the walls of a *jiko* radiate heat in all directions, much of the heat from the fuel is lost to the air. Only half the potential energy of the wood transformed into charcoal is usable in cooking because of losses in carbonization and combustion.

Historical Background for the ATI Project

Research to improve the efficiency of the traditional *jiko* in Kenya began in 1977 at Kenyatta University College and continued at Egerton College. New designs were developed by the Bellerive Foundation in 1979 and by the United

Nations International Children's Fund (UNICEF) in 1980. Public interest in this research was stimulated by a locally organized exhibition that tested charcoal stoves for the UN Conference on New and Renewable Sources of Energy, held in Nairobi in 1981. Subsequently, a large number of organizations sponsored or carried out work to develop, promote, disseminate, and commercialize improved charcoal stoves in Kenya. Key organizations involved in these activities included U.S. Agency for International Development (USAID), the Kenyan Ministry of Energy and Regional Development (MOE), UNICEF,[12] Intermediate Technology Development Group (ITDG), the National Christian Council of Kenya, Appropriate Technology International (ATI), Kenyatta University College, Kenya's Appropriate Technology Advisory Committee, Max Kinyanjui and many other private artisans and distributors.

Initial research focused on two types of design improvements: all-metal stoves and ceramic-lined versions of the traditional *jikos*. Both types accommodate one pot at a time. Although the all-metal stoves were more fuel efficient than the ceramic-lined stoves, they were more expensive and more difficult to use than either the traditional stove or the ceramic-lined *jiko*. In addition, the all-metal stoves were perceived to present a greater danger from burning. As a result of all these factors, only a small number of all-metal stoves were ever sold.

The Kenya Renewable Energy Development Project (KREDP), funded by USAID through MOE, began in September 1981. The improved charcoal stoves components included applied research and prototype development; training, extension and demonstration; development of productive enterprises; and monitoring and evaluation. The improved *jiko* design, which is being adopted in significant numbers and which the ATI project chose to disseminate, is an outgrowth of the KREDP project.

Ceramic-Lined Stoves

Keith Openshaw, a researcher with the Beijer Institute, is credited with introducing, in Kenya in 1981, the idea of adding a ceramic liner to a metal stove—a result of seeing Thai bucket stoves. In mid-1982 (under the KREDP), the Kenyan bucket stove—an adaptation of the Thai bucket stove—was developed. It consisted of a cylindrical, flat-bottomed ceramic liner in a traditional *jiko*. This stove proved to be heavy and difficult to ignite. The liner often cracked and came loose, and the grate broke easily.

The bell-bottom *jiko*, initially developed in late 1983, is similar to other ceramic-lined stoves in that it consists of a metal cladding, a fired ceramic liner and grate, and an insulating layer of cement-vermiculite that binds the liner to the cladding and covers the bottom of the ash box. The metal cladding protects the liner and supports the pots, while the liner reduces heat loss from radiation. The grate aerates the combustion bed and channels heat toward the pot. The insulating layer increases the life of the cladding by reducing its chances of cracking.

In the bell-bottom *jiko*, the one-piece ceramic liner has a perforated floor that serves as a grate. Like a waist, the cladding is narrowest in the middle. This shape allows gravity to hold the liner firmly in place so that it is less prone to cracking from differential expansion in heating. Because the liner extends only halfway down the height, this stove is more portable than the earlier version. It is also cheaper to produce and has a smaller firebox, which reduces the potential for charcoal waste from overloading. The wide bottom of this stove makes it easy to light. The metal pot rests are strong and the wide base is stable during vigorous stirring. The most popular size has a diameter of 28 cm, a height of 28 cm, and a weight of 7 kg. Its fuel efficiency is about 30 percent.

From Research to Introduction of Improved Jikos

The bell-bottom, ceramic-lined *jiko* is the only improved charcoal stove that has been widely accepted in Kenya. Its acceptance can be attributed both to good performance and considerable promotional efforts of the KREDP and private producers.

This design is significantly more efficient than that of the traditional stove, is more compatible with existing cooking methods and is considerably cheaper than the UNICEF (Umeme and Haraka) all-metal stoves (Table 5-2). The spontaneous adoption of the technology by a wide variety of formal and informal manufacturers throughout Nairobi reflects the market for the improved *jiko* and the ease of manufacturing within the existing system. There are, however, technical and financial obstacles to its widespread production and use.

The main technical obstacle is quality control in the production of the ceramic liners. The ceramic liner must be able to withstand temperature changes in cooking (firebox temperatures of over 900° C) and ordinary handling by households. The products of traditional potters in Kenya do not always meet these requirements because they are often fired at lower temperatures.

To achieve the necessary quality, the ceramic liner must be made from a clay substantially modified by the addition of sand and cow dung and must be fired in a permanent kiln to a controlled and consistent temperature. Because the composition and characteristics of clay vary enormously from one deposit to another, the precise mixture of materials must be individually formulated. If the technology is disseminated without careful attention to these factors, the liners will crack easily. Once this problem became known, the design would get a deservedly bad reputation.

Additional obstacles are informational and financial. It took fifty years for the traditional *jiko* to become the dominant cookstove in Kenya. Improved communications and the publicity offered by newspapers, television and radio might halve the amount of time needed to accept the improved *jiko*. Traditional producers—especially those outside of Nairobi—lack the necessary technical support and capital to produce the ceramic-lined stove on a wide scale. Traditional sources of finance such as banks and development finance institutes are unwilling to adapt their criteria to lend to these small and micro-enterprises.

The ATI Project

In mid-1985, ATI approved a three-year grant to the Kenya Energy Non-governmental Organizations Association (KENGO) to accelerate, outside Nairobi, the commercial production and dissemination of the bell-bottom, ceramic-lined *jiko*, work that had begun under the USAID KREDP project. The ATI project was to provide training and technical assistance to enable twenty informal sector manufacturers of traditional *jikos* throughout Kenya to produce the improved ceramic-lined stoves. In addition, support was provided for the development of better methods of clay processing, molding and firing; a publicity and public education campaign; a marketing program; and a quality control certification process. Because small workshops cannot obtain credit from formal sources, a small loan fund was set aside to provide working capital to assist existing potters to build kilns and buy equipment for the production of *jiko* liners.[13]

The technology promoted by the project involved the addition of ceramic liners to the bell-bottom version of the existing traditional *jiko*. There was no doubt that traditional metalworkers would be able to manufacture the cladding for improved *jikos*. They did not need to develop any new skills or depend on any new material input. The risky part of the project involved stimulating the production of a sufficient supply of quality liners.

When the project began, two large and a few small companies were producing the ceramic liners, which were distributed by three suppliers in the capital. Because of the centralized production and distribution strategy, the improved stoves were not widely available outside Nairobi. Furthermore, the dominant market position of the two large producers allowed them to demand a high price for the stoves.[14]

Increasing the availability of the improved *jikos,* at a price affordable by poor households, necessitated a decentralized production strategy. Reliance primarily on existing informal sector metalsmiths and potters was expected to be far less expensive than creation of a centralized industry to produce stoves. Existing commercial channels were to be used to produce and market the improved *jikos*. It was assumed that households would pay a higher price for the improved stove (US$5 versus US$2.50 for the traditional *jiko*) if they were made aware of the overall savings in fuel costs. The present net value of the savings to a Kenyan household using the improved *jikos* for two years is estimated to range from US$16 to US$50, depending on the location (urban, peri-urban or rural) and the market price of charcoal.

Organization of the Project

KENGO, which was chosen to implement the project, specialized in energy and forestry issues. KENGO is a nonprofit consortium of approximately sixty member organizations that operates independently for village and regional development. KENGO carries out demonstration projects and educates Kenyans about the importance of woodlots, bio-gas and improved stoves.

Miaki Jikos, a private partnership, was selected to provide the technical assistance to the improved *jiko* manufacturers. Miaki Jikos had been involved in the production of both metal and ceramic components of the *jikos*. Its proprietor, Max Kinyanjui, was instrumental in promotion and training activities for the bell-bottom *jiko* under the USAID KREDP project.

Technology

The improved stove consists of a clay ceramic liner inserted in a metal *jiko*. Clay has been used as a fire-containing material in stoves for thousands of years. In larger sizes, fired ceramic materials are prone to cracking, because of the stress caused by differential rates of expansion. In smaller dimensions, however, clay often is molded and fired for use in stoves. Free-standing, unsupported clay stoves are commonly used in Southeast Asia, particularly in Thailand, where large quantities are produced in its substantial cottage industries. The applicability of solid clay stoves in Kenya is limited because their manufacture requires relatively sophisticated ceramic technologies and firing systems that are not prevalent in this country. Moreover, such stoves are not easily portable, an important requirement for use in Kenyan urban households.

Metal Claddings

The metal cladding for the improved and traditional *jiko* is manufactured in a similar way. The major difference is that the walls of the improved *jiko* are made in two parts that narrow at the halfway point to produce the appearance of a waist. Templates may be used to cut the metal to ensure consistency. The joint at the center position is folded, a procedure with which local artisans already are familiar. All other attachments, such as pot rest brackets, legs and air door, are riveted. A skilled artisan can produce as many as eight of these new units per day.

Ceramic Liner

The technology to manufacture the liners involves formulation of clay bodies, simple tooling to ensure evenness and regularity and use of an enclosed updraft kiln to control firing temperatures. Producers need to be trained to mold the liners and manage the kiln properly. The production process can be introduced to existing *jiko* makers or taught to local potters, including women's groups. To be well accepted in the market, the liners must be of good quality and readily available.

Producing the liner involves the following steps:[15]

- clay preparation,
- molding with electrical and hand-powered machinery,
- drying, and
- firing in a kiln

Clay Preparation. The most favorable clay mix depends on the type of clays that are locally available. Several types of clays may be used. In some cases, the addition of sawdust significantly reduces cracking by evening out the internal and external rates of drying. The sawdust can increase resistance to thermal shock. As the sawdust is burned in firing, the remaining voids increase the clay's resilience as it expands and contracts. It also may be desirable to add sand to the clay mix.

The traditional method of clay preparation involves crushing and mixing the various clays by foot. Although this is labor intensive and an inexpensive method of production, the resulting mixture may be uneven. A mechanical pulverizer is desirable, but not necessary.

A pug mill also may be helpful in attaining high-quality liners, but this equipment is expensive. A pug mill operates at a very slow speed and homogenizes the mix of materials—harder and softer clays, sawdust and sand—into a unified body of even consistency. It helps maintain the correct proportion of water to ensure plasticity and ease of molding. In Kenya, a locally manufactured pug mill costs approximately US$6,000. Its capacity is approximately 660 kg of clay per hour.

Molding Equipment (jigger jolly). A skilled worker who has received six months of on-the-job training can produce about thirty liners per day by hand. But the liner sizes can be inconsistent and consumers may not like the handmade appearance. Furthermore, when dry, hand-molded liners have a high cracking rate—about 30 percent.

Because the high cracking rate might significantly impede the adoption of the improved *jikos,* an ATI staff engineer, Hugh Allen, designed a mechanized jigger jolly that increases the production rate and the uniformity of the molding and reduces cracking rates substantially. The machine is able to produce one hundred and twenty liners a day. The machine-made liners have a much smoother appearance than the hand-molded type and the cracking rates have been reduced from 30 percent to 10 percent.

Drying. The liners must be dried in the shade for one week. The way the liners are stacked is important. If they are stacked on top of each other or turned upside down to dry, the cracking rate will be at least 10 percent higher. When each liner is set out to dry individually, the cracking rate is reduced to 2 percent.

Kiln Construction and Firing. The best type of kiln for firing is the up-draft kiln, made from common red bricks, with underfloor heating over firebars which can reach a temperature of 750°–800° C. An updraft kiln will use approximately 200 kg of dry firewood to fire four hundred and forty liners in four and a half hours. Liner loss rates in the kiln average 1.5 percent. In comparison, a down-draft kiln consumes approximately 500 kg of wood and can fire two hundred liners in ten hours.

Marketing

In general, the informal sector offers work opportunities with few entry barriers. Although lack of capital is a constraint, the low levels of skill required in most informal sector activities generate intense competition.

The introduction of a pug mill and jigger jolly to ensure quality standards, two relatively expensive pieces of equipment, did increase the entry barriers significantly for the informal sector artisans. Yet, the mechanization and standardization of the product helped lower the price of the improved *jiko*. When the stove was first introduced, it was priced as high as KSh250. By mid-1988, however, the ex-factory price was KSh60–65 and the retail price averaged KSh70–85.[16]

As the technology becomes standardized and more widely adopted, and informal sector *jiko* producers obtain access to capital to invest in the required machinery, competition could lower the price even more. A preliminary commercial analysis indicates that the stove can be produced for as little as KSh52–60.

The most popular traditional *jiko*, which is significantly less energy efficient than the improved *jiko,* retails for KSh40 or 60 percent of the price of the improved stove. To convince traditional *jiko* users, especially in rural areas, of the fuel savings possible with the improved *jiko,* KENGO undertook a public information and education campaign that focused on household energy conservation. Articles were written for local newspapers and for KENGO's own newsletter; a video, "How to Make the Kenya Ceramic *Jiko,*" was produced to train artisans. Slide/tape shows on Kenya's fuelwood crisis and on improved *jikos* were produced and shown in the schools. Radio programs in both English and Kiswahili were especially effective in promoting the use of the improved *jiko.*

Conclusions

By 1988, largely as a result of the USAID, KREDP and ATI projects, more than 200,000 improved *jikos* had been produced and sold. But the process that led to this success has evolved differently from that originally envisioned. A number of interesting lessons can be learned from this experience.

Effectiveness and Efficiency of R&D Efforts

Several organizations have invested considerable time and money in R&D on household charcoal stoves in Kenya. Several designs for both all-metal *jikos* and ceramic-lined *jikos* were tested simultaneously. The all-metal stoves promoted by UNICEF never became commercially popular. The ceramic-lined stoves gained in popularity as the price was lowered, but some difficulties were encountered in commercial production—especially in making the ceramic lining of the *jikos*. Faulty liners, which adversely affected the stove's efficiency and durability, began to give the stove design a bad reputation.

Three factors are critical in production of the ceramic liner: the clay quality, the molding of the liner and the firing. Two approaches were tried to solve these problems. The first approach emphasized training artisans in clay selection and molding. The second approach, instituted by ATI, was to mechanize the production of liners. Mechanization of clay preparation and molding resulted in a more standardized product, but the cost of the necessary equipment (the pug mill and jigger jolly) limited production to a few medium-scale enterprises.

Training

Training can be slow and costly, especially for artisans who are just beginning stove production. The impact of the training programs was very poor.[17] Unfortunately, only a small proportion of the trainers were effective. Poorly paid trainers often quit their jobs after a short period of time to begin producing *jikos* themselves—a more lucrative opportunity. The trainees often complained that they could not obtain ceramic liners, sufficient capital or orders for the improved *jikos*. Moreover, few of the artisans had sufficient management or marketing skills. As a result, artisans outside Nairobi continued to make traditional *jikos* or relocated to the capital, thus defeating one of the purposes of the project, to decentralize the production of improved *jikos*.

Quality control proved to be a problem for the ceramic liners, but not for the metal claddings. The quality problem could eventually have been solved through competition, which would have driven low-quality producers out of the market. But this also could have damaged the reputation of the improved design and slowed consumer acceptance.

The recent introduction of the pug mill, the jigger jolly and other recommended changes in the technology for making ceramic liners reduced quality control problems and expanded production, thus also reducing domestic charcoal consumption. This equipment, however, requires higher capital investment. Thus, it is likely that liner production will be dominated by a few medium-size firms in Nairobi and a few others in areas such as Mombasa, Kisumu and around Mt. Kenya. Decentralized liner production appears possible only in areas where there is a strong tradition of pottery making; this is not the case in Western Kenya. Larger, more centralized urban producers have better access to suitable raw materials and can arrange sale and transport of their liners more easily than can small, rural producers.

Financial Concerns

Although the improved *jikos* are rapidly being accepted by traditional *jiko* users, the improved stoves are not yet being used by those people who need them most—the rural and urban poor. Most purchasers to date have come from the middle and lower middle classes, in urban areas. Low-income households, which have pressing needs for cash, cannot afford the higher capital outlay for the improved stove (US$5 for the improved *jiko* versus US$2.50 for the traditional *jiko*), even if this would result in a net savings over the long run. The net present value (NPV) over a two-year period to a household adopting an improved *jiko* ranges from KSh257 to KSh884 if charcoal is purchased in tins, or KSh109 to KSh518 if charcoal is purchased in sacks.

In retrospect, one must question ATI's decision to finance improvements in the quality of production by introducing the pug mill and the jigger jolly, without also designing a plan to allow users to finance the purchase of the improved stove.

The lack of availability of replacement liners, especially in rural areas, also hindered rapid adaptation of the improved *jikos* by the poor. On the occasions when improved *jikos* were available in rural areas, the poor people did not buy them. Buying an all-new, improved *jiko*—rather than replacing the liner—represents a significant additional expenditure for the poor.

The project's experience with Kenyan charcoal stoves is important because it shows how a market can function in spreading a new technology. Despite the intention to reach the rural market (towns), the main market for *jikos* is still in the cities where the largest concentration of charcoal users congregate. And, even though over the long run the urban poor would find the improved *jiko* to be most economical, most purchasers to date have come from the middle and lower-middle classes.

A number of issues are related to the question of production *by* the masses versus production *for* the masses. Two objectives of this effort came into conflict. National energy conservation was the primary objective; rural employment was a second objective. Originally, the intention was to produce *jikos by* the masses (local artisans in rural areas). However, if the improved *jiko* was to be widely accepted, a good quality product was required. Thus production *for* the masses by a few artisans in urban areas turned out to be more practical.

Given the environmental objectives, would it have made sense to donate the improved *jikos* and subsidize the purchase of replacement liners? This step would have increased local savings or increased local spendable income in turn generating demand for other products. Subsidies for charcoal users could reduce pressures on scarce wood resources. This could, however, have a counterproductive effect by encouraging users of firewood, kerosene or liquid propane gas fuels to switch to charcoal, and thus increase overall wood consumption. A careful analysis of Kenyan energy consumption is important in answering the question.

Unlike other cases discussed in this book, in which ATI helped create demand by assisting the buyers to finance their purchases, this project focused on introducing standardized production methods to obtain a good quality product. This approach has been successful even though poorer users still have not been reached in large numbers.

Notes

1. Eric Hyman, "The Strategy of Production and Distribution of Imported Charcoal Stoves in Kenya," *World Development* 15(3) 1987, pp. 375–380.

2. Hugh Allen et al., "Ceramic Lined *Jikos*," *Project Plan ATI* (Washington, D.C.: Appropriate Technology International, 1985), p. 4.

3. In 1980, there were 156,000 hectares (ha) of woodlots and periurban plantations in Kenya yielding an average of 16.1 ton of wood/ha and 166,700 ha of managed productive forests yielding 4.9 ton/ha. Assuming that both types of forest are the source for additional supplies of wood for charcoal making in proportion to their current annual

yields, an 80 percent adoption rate for improved *jikos* in 1985 would have eliminated the need to clear 45,300 ha of woodlots and periurban plantations as well as 47,800 ha of managed productive forests each year. In the year 2000, the annual savings would be 163,000 ha of woodlots and 172,600 ha of managed forests. See also O'Keefe, Raskin and Bernow in Eric Hyman, *World Development,* p. 375, on this topic.

4. Potential national savings at national level are indicated below:

Aggregate Annual Cash Savings on Charcoal at Different
Rates of Adoption, Including Replacement Cost

At 10% rate of adoption	KSh26,496,000
20%	54,992,000
60%	164,768,000
75%	205,960,000
80%	219,691,000

Source: Project Plan ATI, p. 19.

5. Eric Hyman, "The Economics of Improved Charcoal Stoves in Kenya," *Energy Policy,* p. 150.

6. Hyman, p. 150.

7. KSh700–800 = US$41–$47. Note: Exchange rate KSh17 = US$1 International Financial Statistics (IFS) 47(10) (October 1988).

8. Gross national product USD 300 = US$300. *World Bank Report* (Oxford: Oxford University Press, 1988).

9. The largest concentration of informal sector metalsmiths in Nairobi is at the Shauri Moyo market. Although no data are available on the number of these enterprises or the number of artisans involved, it would take approximately 1,000 artisans to supply the total national market, assuming that each artisan spends about one third of his time making *jikos* (1000 X 7 units per day X 0.333 day X 250 days per year = 583,000 units).

10. Stephen Joseph, Yvonne Shanahan and Peter Young, "The Performance of Kenyan Charcoal Stoves" (London: Intermediate Technology Development Group, 1982), in Hyman, *Energy Policy,* p. 153.

11. Max Kinyanjui, personal communication (1985), in Hyman, *Energy Policy,* p. 153.

12. Sambali and Schneiders, 1984; *UNICEF Technology Support Section, UNICEF Stoves,* n.d.

13. *Project Plan ATI,* p. 9–11.

14. *Project Plan ATI,* p. 9–11.

15. The section on technology draws heavily upon the material of Hugh Allen, "Project Brief: The Technology of Ceramic Lined Charcoal Stove Production: Mechanized Production in Kenya," Nairobi, 1988, p. 3–16.

16. Sylvester A. Namuye, *Survey on Dissemination and Impact of Kenya Ceramic Jiko in Kenya* (Nairobi: Energy and Environment Organizations, July 1987), pp. 40–42.

17. Hyman, Eric, "The Strategy of Production and Distribution of Improved Charcoal Stoves in Kenya," *World Development* 15(3) 1987, pp. 375–386.

6 Commercializing Small-Scale Production of Pigs in the Dominican Republic

FOR ALL HIS FIFTY-THREE YEARS, ANTONIO SANCHEZ has lived in the small mountain village of Licey. On his 3.5-hectare plot, he grows coffee, beans and cassava and raises a few chickens. Antonio also raises pigs, his major source of cash income.

Until ten years ago, Antonio did not consider pig farming a business. Because his cash investment was minimal, he kept no records on the costs incurred to raise the *criollo,* or native, pigs. He bred his *criollo* pigs on his farm and fed them scraps and farm-grown produce. When he needed cash, he sold a pig or two.

In 1978, African swine fever swept through the Dominican Republic; all his pigs had to be slaughtered. The replacement pigs that he obtained through a newly created farmer's association—the Moca Farmers Association—were much larger than the *criollo* pigs. The association told Antonio that these genetically improved pigs would need a balanced diet, including feed supplements, if they were to thrive. The expenses incurred for purchased feeds meant that Antonio no longer could consider his pigs a subsistence bonus; now his pigs were an investment.

Antonio became active in the Moca Farmers Association. Through it he was

This chapter was researched and written by Stijntje Schreurs and John Skibiak, in association with Ton de Wilde.

able to obtain relatively inexpensive high protein feed that he uses to supplement feeds available on his farm. He learned new techniques in swine production, such as improved methods of penning and the importance of veterinary medicines.

Antonio is earning more money from the sale of pigs than he did previously, and credits most of his good fortune to the fact that he joined the association. As a member, he receives up-to-the minute information on pork and feed prices —information that is critical in an economy subject to government devaluations of the peso coupled with price controls on pork. He no longer considers his pigs an emergency bank account. For the first time in his life, he has a bank account that he can draw upon in case of emergencies. Antonio looks upon his pigs as an investment to generate income for years to come.

The Destruction of Subsistence Pig-Raising Activities

Swine production in the Dominican Republic came to an abrupt halt in 1978 with the outbreak of an African swine fever epidemic. The disease, which is transmitted through direct contact and ingestion of contaminated wastes, spread quickly throughout the island of Hispaniola. Because there is no known vaccine or cure, the Dominican Republic government had no option but to order an immediate slaughter of its entire swine population. By mid-1980, nearly two million pigs had been killed in a less than twelve months.

Before the epidemic, well over 70 percent of all swine production in the Dominican Republic had been carried out at the household level, most of it for subsistence. Recognizing the potential impact this epidemic could have on such a large segment of its population, the Dominican Republic government quickly took action to rebuild the national swine herd. Its strategy involved importing genetically improved pigs from the United States (some of which were donated under the U.S. foreign assistance program).

These imported pigs had a high efficiency ratio in converting feed into meat. But they maintain this efficiency only if fed a balanced diet containing protein, vitamins and minerals. The imported pigs were allocated to large-scale producers and rural associations, many of which were established solely for the purpose of receiving pigs. The repopulation effort progressed rapidly. By the end of 1983, imported pigs and their offspring numbered at least 100,000. While prospects looked good for the repopulation effort, other changes, caused by the deteriorating economic condition of the country, were taking place that would profoundly affect the future of swine production in the Dominican Republic.

The Political Economy of the Dominican Republic

The Dominican Republic, with a population of 6.4 million, occupies the eastern two-thirds of Hispaniola, the second largest island in the Caribbean. Its gross national product (GNP) per capita of US$710 (1988)[1] places it among the developing world's middle-income economies. During the presidency of Joaquin Balaguer (1966–1978), the Dominican Republic averaged an economic growth rate of nearly 7 percent per annum. Since 1980, however, real living standards have fallen (Table 6–1).

Table 6-1 Income per Capita, Dominican Republic, 1960–88

	1960	*1970*	*1980*	*1988*
Population (in thousands)	3,047	4,006	5,431	6,400
GDP per capita (1980 US$)	625	780	1,124	710
	1960–1970		*1970–1980*	*1980–1988*
Annual average growth rates of per capita income (percent)	2.2		6.0	-4.2

Source: K. J. Coutts, H. Guiliani Cury and F. Pellerano, "Stabilisation Programmes and Structural Adjustment Policies in the Dominican Republic," in *Labour and Society* (Geneva: International Labor Organization, 1986), p. 362. Data are adjusted to 1988.

Although the Dominican Republic until recently has been largely self-sufficient in food,[2] it must import many other commodities like energy (oil), machinery, and transport equipment. The Dominican Republic is heavily dependent on the United States. Sixty percent of its exports (in 1985, US$735 million) go to the United States. The Dominican Republic's export revenues are still dominated by four traditional commodities: sugar (from sugar cane), coffee, cocoa and tobacco. Income from exports, a fast-growing tourism industry and the money sent back by Dominicans who are working in the United States represent the main sources of foreign exchange.

By 1981, a collapse in sugar prices and an increase in oil prices had dealt heavy blows to the Dominican Republic's economy. When Jorge Blanco became president in 1981, he faced an external debt of US$2.2 billion, which was 39.4 percent of gross domestic product (GDP).[3]

Negotiations were started with the International Monetary Fund (IMF) and the U.S. Economic Support Fund to alleviate the country's financial and economic problems. In January 1983, a three-year IMF stabilization program released approximately US$450 million in short-term credit. This agreement called for implementation of a variety of austerity measures starting in April 1984.[4]

- Nearly all non-oil import payments were to be made at the market rate of foreign exchange instead of the official exchange rate, which was artificially held at 1:1.
- Exporters of the country's traditional goods—sugar, coffee, cocoa,

tobacco, gold, silver and ferronickel—were offered a revised exchange rate of 1.48 Dominican Republic pesos per US$1 instead of the previous rate of RDP1.

- Inflation was to be contained by limiting public sector spending.

Decreased subsidies for staple foods resulted in massive price increases. For example, the price of bread increased by 35 percent, sugar by 17 percent and cooking oil by 100 percent. With an inflation rate estimated to be between 24 percent to 40 percent, the average real income of farmers fell to approximately US$350 annually, less than half the average annual GNP per capita in 1978. Unemployment rates of at least 30 percent reduced private and public investment, and a reduction in government services led to a decline in domestic standards of living. The situation resulted in serious public demonstrations and riots.

Negotiations to extend austerity measures into a second year were terminated, largely due to the government's reluctance to calculate the price of petroleum imports at the market exchange rate, which would have resulted in higher costs to importers and consumers. In response, the Fund canceled its stabilization program.

In August 1984, after long negotiation with the IMF and the World Bank (WB), the Dominican Republic government initiated a transitional program, known as the Shadow Program. Its purpose was to borrow time to formulate new policies and maintain the flow of U.S. aid to the country. Part of the program included a 70 percent (approximate) increase in petroleum prices. In April 1985, the IMF approved a RDP75.5 million standby agreement with the Dominican Republic. The stated objectives of the program were to further strengthen the country's balance-of-payments position, to reduce inflationary pressure, to reduce the public sector deficit, and to create the conditions for renewed growth. When the standby agreement expired in April 1986, all quantitative performance criteria had been met by a considerable margin, with the exception of the balance-of-payments current account target.

In May 1986, declining economic conditions may have helped re-elect the then seventy-eight-year-old Joaquin Balaguer, whom voters associated with an image of better times. But an unstable economy cannot be corrected by one person. By March 1988, the foreign debt had increased to RDP4 billion; violent anti-government protests and strikes to end rising prices and low wages broke out. In June 1988, all banks closed for a few days when the peso was devalued from RDP6.40 to RDP8.20 to the U.S. dollar. As a result, food prices again increased significantly. In an effort to reduce the adverse impact of the devaluation on the very poor, the government established special markets, Plazas Populares, where staple foods could be purchased at subsidized prices.

Impact of the Macroeconomic Environment on Pig Producers

The macroeconomic environment has had a great impact on swine producers, who are mostly small-scale farmers. First, the increased supply of pigs led to a substantial drop in the domestic price of pork. Between 1982 and 1984, pork prices per kilo dropped from RDP3.59 to a low of RDP2.40—a decrease that in real terms exceeded 33 percent.[5]

Table 6-2   Net Income from Swine Production in the Dominican Republic in RDP 1982–85

Year	Production and Marketing Costs per 95-kg Pig	Pork Price/kg to Farmer	Gross Net Income	Income
1982	160.94	2.70	256.50	95.56
1983	158.69	2.60	247.00	88.31
1984	212.69	2.55	242.25	29.56
1985	302.71	3.20	304.00	1.29

Source: Secretaria de Estado Agricultura, Dirección General de Gauaderia, *Situación y Perspectivas de la Producción Porcina en la República Dominicana* (Santo Domingo, 1985).

Second, the introduction of IMF-inspired austerity measures in 1985 led to a gradual devaluation of the Dominican Republic peso and a commensurate increase in the price of imported animal feed. Because feed costs represent at least 80 percent of swine production costs, the profitability of swine production decreased sharply. It is estimated that net income from swine production dropped by nearly 99 percent between 1982 and 1985 (see Table 6-2).

The third development to influence local swine production was the dramatic change required in animal husbandry techniques. To the small-scale farmer, the criollo pig represented a cost-free source of meat. *Criollo* pigs required little capital investment and ate kitchen wastes and other farm-grown produce. By contrast, a completely new set of production techniques was needed to raise the genetically improved pigs. These pigs required nutritionally balanced feeds, which, when produced commercially, contained costly protein components, usually soybean. Furthermore, there was greater need for sophisticated penning equipment, feeding troughs, veterinary attention, antibiotics and other items not generally used by small-scale farmers.

These changes and the outlay of cash they necessitated transformed the role of livestock production in the household economy. Previously, the low-cost feeding regimen of the *criollo* pig had enabled farmers to maintain livestock indefinitely or at least until the animals were slaughtered for domestic consumption. Alternatively, livestock holdings served as a source of cash for emergencies, for example, if a family member needed medicine or needed to pay for special family occasions.

Ongoing expenses for purchased feeds and ancillary equipment effectively prohibited farmers from maintaining the imported pigs as a subsistence activity. The continual cash outlay for commercial feed, for instance, required producers to sell pigs at an optimal weight—the point (approximately 100 kg) after which further feed inputs would not yield proportional returns on their investment in the pig. To the small farmer, therefore, the subsistence orientation of rural swine production was as much a victim of the swine fever epidemic as was the native *criollo* pig itself.

By 1984, many of the farmer associations established during the initial repopulation effort had begun distributing breeding stock directly to individual members. Many farmers found it difficult—both financially and technically—to raise the genetically improved swine breeds. Pigs became sick as farmers tried substituting household refuse and other farm-grown foods (the same items they had given to their *criollo* pigs) for the often prohibitively expensive commercial feeds. Geographic isolation made it difficult for the farmers to obtain commercial feed at any price. Feed distribution networks were poorly developed and farmers had to travel long distances to obtain the expensive feed. The consequences of these conditions were soon evident.

Between 1984 and 1985, the number of swine-producing units in the Dominican Republic decreased by at least 31 percent (Table 6-3). Most of these (86 percent) were small units, farmers who had fewer than twenty-five pigs. In some provinces, such as La Vega, household swine production disappeared completely, despite widespread farmer participation in the government's swine repopulation program.

Table 6-3 Decrease in Number of Swine-Producing Units (1984–85)

| Region | No. of Units, July 1984 | No. of Units, June 1985 | Percentage Decrease | Percentage of Total Decrease by Size of Unit | |
				< = 25 pigs	> = 25 pigs
Northeast	1,373	975	29	100	0
North	2,446	1,688	31	93	7
North central	1,441	1,008	30	89	12
Central	769	546	29	50	50
East	951	570	40	100	0
Total	6,980	4,787	31.4 %	86.4%	13.8%

Source: Censo Porcino Julio 1984 y *Muestro Porcino* Junio 1985, *Dirección General de Ganaderia* (Santo Domingo, 1985), Annexes 2, 4.

Introduction of the Project

Given the bleak prospects for small-scale swine production in the Dominican Republic, Associated Technology International (ATI) and the Center of Investigation and Improvement of Animal Production (CIMPA), a local, private, nonprofit organization dedicated to improving livestock production in the northern half of the Dominican Republic, launched an experimental program in 1984. The goal of the project was to develop and test a commercially viable technology delivery system that would provide small swine producers in the Central

Cibao Region access to high-protein feed and medicine. To reduce feed costs, high-value feeds would be replaced with selected farm refuse and feed components that could be produced on the farm. Farmers were expected to benefit in two ways: profits of those families already involved in commercial swine production would increase, and families who had only kept pigs only on a subsistence basis would now be able to afford commercial swine production for the first time. The goal of the project was to raise the annual real income of at least 2,000 farmers by 18 percent.

The core of the project design was an innovative technology package that enabled farmers to prepare their own nutritionally balanced feeds using low-cost purchased inputs, and feeds already available on the farm. The package consisted of two components. The first was a feed based on a laboratory-tested formula for preparing balanced swine feeds together with three new feed, or reference, inputs—ramie, a green fodder to be used as a protein supplement; molasses, a byproduct of sugar production to provide energy; and a 40 percent protein concentrate composed of soybean meal, minerals and supplemental amino acids and vitamins. When combined in the recommended proportions, the new swine feed was expected to cost considerably less than traditional commercial feeds. The package's second component was a delivery system that established local marketing networks to distribute the molasses and protein concentrate.

By the end of 1985, economic changes forced a change in the project's farm-based feed component. Ramie proved to be no less seasonal than any other green fodder. After government subsidies for sugar were removed, molasses became far too expensive.[6] Almost overnight, the wholesale price of molasses jumped from RDP13 to RDP85 per gallon, causing the retail price to soar to RDP150. The 40 percent protein supplement was never popular among farmers. Both Campesinos Federados de Salcedo (CAFESA) and Asociación para el Desarrollo de la Provincia Espaillat (Association for Development in Espaillat Province, Dominican Republic (ADEPE)), which possessed equipment for processing feed, responded by offering farmers a wider range of feed inputs such as wheat, maize, sorghum and rice bran, as well as locally produced balanced feeds.

In response to these changes, in 1986 the project adopted a new feeding strategy. Because it was not available year round, ramie was dropped from the list of reference inputs. The revised project no longer prescribed a specific feed formula, but shifted to a new feeding strategy subsequently dubbed the cafeteria approach, whereby farmers would supplement commercial feeds with selected farm produce.

Needs and Obstacles to the Commercialization of Subsistence Pig Raising

Today, a wide range of pig-producing activities are carried out in the Dominican Republic. The attitudes toward swine production and the marketing of pork in the Dominican Republic have changed substantially. Pork is produced by different groups—individual farmers, associations and middle- and large-scale producers—each of which was affected differently.

The Traditional Market

In the Dominican Republic, many small-scale farmers live a subsistence existence. They often cultivate a small plot of land outside their village where they grow coffee, beans, corn, potatoes and cassava, and usually maintain some livestock, such as chickens and pigs. Before the African swine fever epidemic, raising pigs required minimal investment. When a farmer wanted to sell a pig, he informed the buyer, who would come with his truck to the mountain village. Even when demand was low, the farmer could easily keep his pig for a couple of months with few additional costs.

Current Market Forces

In theory, the Dominican Republic has a free market economy in which prices are a function of supply and demand. However, because a large percentage of the food supply is imported, any devaluation of the Dominican Republic peso directly affects the ability of the rural poor to afford essential purchases. For this reason the government has found it necessary in the past to intervene by artificially fixing prices for essential food items, including pork. For farmers, this policy has at times meant a drastic drop in pork profits from one day to the next. Although the price of pork is constrained by what the consumer can (or will) pay, production costs (of which feed is the principal component) reflect the real prices of imported ingredients.

For most small-scale farmers living in the mountains, a lack of up-to-date information on feed and pork prices greatly hinders effective management of commercial swine production. To make matters worse, farmers must obtain such information from the very people who can use it to their own advantage, the traders. Previously, farmers would maintain a few extra pigs indefinitely as a kind of personal savings account. Today, however, unless they keep track of both changing prices for imported feed and the sales price for pork, they can quickly wind up in debt.

The introduction of genetically improved pig breeds created a new industry in the Dominican Republic. What was once a subsistence activity now required some investment. With the commercialization of this activity, the demand structure changed, prompting more middle- and large-scale producers to enter the market. Competition was thereby increased.

Middle- and Large-Scale Industries

Although the introduction of the genetically improved pig made swine production an organized and profitable enterprise, to achieve high profitability relatively large investments are required.[7] Not only are the pigs more expensive (a newly weaned pig costs RDP100–120, whereas a *criollo* piglet had cost RDP$5), but raising them to their optimal weight of 100 kg costs a farmer an additional

RDP274 (1988 prices). The optimal weight is reached after six months (see Table 6-4).

Table 6-4   Production Costs of a 100-kg Pig (May 1988)

Purchase of a newly weaned pig[a]	RDP110.00
Feeding (5.6 cwt of concentrated feed at RDP49.00/cwt)	RDP274.40
Others (pig pen/handling equipment)[b]	RDP15.00
Total Cost	RDP399.40

[a] Current market price. Most farmers, however, raise their own piglets. In that case, the cost involves feed for the female pig during gestation and lactation, which is slightly less than the cost at market price.
[b] The price for pig pens and handling equipment is based on a material cost of RDP100 over a five-year life, adjusted for inflation.
Source: Jose Luis Rojas, Commercial-Economic Evaluation: "Swine Feed Delivery System for Small Farmers," in *Evaluation Report for ATI* (Santiago, Dominican Republic: CIMPA, 1987). Mimeograph. Prices adjusted by Jose Luis Rojas to reflect situation as of May 1988.

In the northern part of the country, including the Central Cibao Region, which accounts for about 64.4 percent of the Dominican Republic's total swine production,[8] the three most important large-scale producers of pigs are Asociación Porcicultores de Cibao (APORCI) in La Vega, Cooperación Nacionál de Productores de Cerdos (COONA-PROCE) in Moca and Asociación de Porcicultores de Licey (APORLI) in Licey.

Most traders prefer to deal with these large-scale producers, because their location near urban centers considerably reduces transport costs. Supply is assured, and there is a likelihood of better quality pork because the large-scale producers are less likely than small farmers to adulterate commercial feeds with on-farm fillers.

Small-Scale Producers

From a purely economic point of view, one might argue that the swine production industry would be most efficiently handled by large-scale producers. Not only do they benefit from economies of scale, but they are also in a better financial position to obtain credit. Their standing with government officials also helps them to obtain special personal subsidies for which the small isolated farmers would be ineligible.

Despite these factors, pig raising can be very profitable even for the small farmer. First, the opportunity costs for rural labor are minimal. Second, agricultural wastes available on the farm can meet most of the pig's feed requirements.

Nevertheless, small-scale swine production requires significant changes in the way farmers have traditionally produced pork. For one thing, there is a major difference between subsistence farming that entails hardly any investment (RDP5 per pig) or risk, and for-profit commercial farming. As shown in

Table 6-4, raising genetically improved pigs entails a substantial investment as well as risk on the part of the small farmer. Farmers must change their entire attitude toward pig production. They must learn that investments are necessary if they are to make a reasonable profit. They must develop more contacts with the outside world or at least improve their access to current and reliable information on local market conditions. They must change their view of pigs from that of an emergency savings fund to that of a commercial operation.

The riskiest part of raising pigs is the feed component. Funds for small investments, such as pig pens, can be borrowed from friends. Most of these pens, in fact, are built by the farmers themselves.[9] The pigs themselves need not be bought as they can be bred on the farm. But the high-protein feeds, vitamins and medicines must be bought in the nearest city, where the feed processing enterprises are located. Three such enterprises in the Central Cibao Region offer feed at different prices and also offer different services (Table 6-5). The companies process the feed from imported corn and soybean meal, as well as from locally available feed ingredients such as wheat.

Table 6-5   Prices of Feed by Different Feed-Processing Companies[a]

Type of feed[b]	Alimentos Balanceados	APORLI	Cooperación
Gestation	RDP 52.00	RDP 51.00	RDP 51.50
Lactating	57.00	55.00	56.00
Starter	69.00	65.00	63.00
Grower	60.00	56.00	57.00
Finishing	56.00	52.00	54.50

[a] Prices per quintile (100 lb.), June 1988.
[b] By June 1988, prices of all imported products had increased dramatically. Though the increase was abnormally high, it only illustrates more clearly the vulnerability of the small farmer.
Source: Jose Luis Rojas, Commercial-Economic Evaluation: "Swine Feed Delivery System for Small Farmers," in *Evaluation Report for ATI,* CIMPA, Santiago, Dominican Republic, 1987. Mimeograph. Prices adjusted by Rojas to reflect situation as of May, 1988.

Alimentos Balanceados, one of the feed enterprises, is authorized to purchase imported feed items at subsidized prices (it can buy wheat for US$12.50 rather than for the market price of US$45 per ton). It typically provides to farmers credit that can either be repaid in cash or with pigs raised to the required weight of 100 kg. It also transports the feed to the villages. In contrast, the Moca Farmers Association has no access to government subsidies, nor does it offer credit or transport services.

Because few feed processing companies can offer the service provided by Alimentos Balanceados, farmers have found it beneficial to cooperate with each other to buy the feed in bulk. Transport costs per unit are lower, and by visiting the town to get their feed they can collect information on prices and markets.

Fluctuations in the world price for coffee and the lack of alternative income-generating opportunities have made pig raising an economic necessity for most small-scale farmers (Table 6-6). Without this supplemental source of cash income, in emergencies farmers would have to borrow at the usurious rates of the informal credit market.

Table 6-6   Annual Incomes of Farmers in RDP (1987)

1. Annual income without additional income-generating activity:

Coffee harvesting season	RDP1,500.00
(3 months at $500/month)	
Season without coffee harvesting [a]	RDP450.00
(9 months at $50/month)	
Total income/year	RDP1,950.00

2. Annual income including the pig-raising activity:

Income from coffee and other activities [b]	RDP1,950.00
Net income from selling two pigs	
(100 kg each) a year [c]	RDP284.00
Total income/year	RDP2,234.00

[a] Period from January to September. In this season the farmer gets involved in different harvesting and paid labor activities.
[b] The harvest is in October, November and December. Most small farmers have side activities as paid laborers; they sell coffee and/or get jobs, together with their families, as paid laborers.
[c] The sale price is RDP4.20/kg. The calculated production cost of the pig is RDP278.00.
Source: Jose Luis Rojas, "Commercial-Economic Evaluation: Swine Feed Delivery System for Small Farmers," in *Evaluation Report for ATI,* CIMPA, Santiago, Dominican Republic, 1987. Mimeograph. Prices adjusted by Rojas to reflect situation as of May, 1988.

Credit for Small-Scale Farmers

Any farmer wishing to engage in swine production needs initial capital to buy young pigs (later they can be bred), penning equipment, feed, vitamins and medicines. In the Dominican Republic, the Banco Agricola de la República Dominicana (BARD) is the only official source of credit for agricultural and livestock purposes. As in most countries, Dominican banks are reluctant to provide details on their loan portfolio. The most one can expect is a general statement outlining the requirements for credit. In theory, every applicant must be at least eighteen years old, in good health, have knowledge of business administration, be known to the bank and have the necessary commercial qualifications.

The BARD provides loans up to a maximum of RDP100,000, but it has a special loan scheme for farmers who raise pigs. Applicants are divided into three groups; each group must meet a different set of loan conditions.

1. Farmers who need money for medicines and other equipment receive a grace period of six months and have a maximum of two years to repay the loan.
2. Farmers who wish to expand production receive a grace period of one year during which interest accrues, but need not be repaid. The payback period for the loan is four years.
3. Farmers who wish to start raising pigs receive a grace period of one year during which interest accrues, but need not be repaid. The payback period for the loan is nine years.

The following conditions apply to all groups:

1. Farmers must be able to demonstrate to the bank that their farms will remain profitable while the pig-raising activity is carried out.
2. Because the bank will finance only initial investments, not recurrent costs, farmers must have enough resources to raise and maintain imported pigs.
3. Collateral is required, except for first-time borrowers. In these cases the pigs will function as collateral. These unsecured loans cannot exceed RDP20,000.
4. The interest rate is 12 percent annually, but a service fee of 2 percent is levied on top of each payment.

Any association that applies for a loan must present to the bank the following documents that attest to the group's legal status and formal composition:

- Articles of incorporation
- Minutes of the meeting of the constitutive assembly
- Name of the local or national periodical where the incorporation of the association has been published
- A certified copy of the act of incorporation
- Names and personal information of the officers of the association
- Financial records

Though bank officials view these conditions as particularly favorable to the small-scale pig producers, it appears that only one association had ever applied for a loan. Moreover, the loan was not for pig production, but for coffee cultivation.

Observations made by the project staff indicate that farmers must cross a threshold, both psychologically as well as in terms of financial success, before they will go to a bank to apply for a loan. The biases of bank personnel against lending to what is perceived as a risky sector of society is confirmed by studies done elsewhere.[10]

Formalizing Backyard Swine Production

The rebuilding of the national swine herd from 1980 to 1986 in a sense forced Dominican peasant farmers into a new game, the rules of which they did not fully understand. If they played well, the new system allowed farmers to reap substantial profits. If they played poorly, which was more often the case during the early years, farmers lost badly. Between 1985 and 1987, for example, weaner pig mortality rates soared from 25 percent to 50 percent.[11] A major factor in the increase of the mortality rate was the tendency for farmers to respond to cost increases in commercial feed by randomly substituting the on-farm produce and household wastes previously fed to their *criollo* pigs. One observer described the transition as forcing people who had relied for generations on a traditional saving system—their *criollo* pigs—to play the stock market, without even knowing what stocks were.

The following section describes in detail how CIMPA and ATI worked to transform pig raising from an informal subsistence activity to a formal, commercially viable activity.

CIMPA: The Implementing Organization

The project is administered and coordinated by CIMPA, a private, nonprofit organization dedicated to improving livestock production in the northern half of the Dominican Republic. CIMPA is affiliated with the Development Association of Santiago (OAS), one of the first such associations established in Latin America, and is financed by both private and government sources. Technical assistance is provided by two government organizations, the National Center for Animal Investigation (CENIP) and the National Swine Repopulation Program. Commercial credit accounts are held and managed locally by selected provincial development. Of the six such associations in the Cibao region, three participated in the project. These associations are modeled after the Development Association of Santiago and are private voluntary groups controlled by civic-minded businesspeople and professionals principally concerned with the socioeconomic development of their province.

The project is both supply and demand oriented. Commercial credit was provided to selected local vendors to assure that adequate local supplies of the referenced feed inputs could be maintained. Because these inputs are not typically available in rural areas, potential local vendors of agricultural inputs such as farmer cooperatives, agricultural supply stores, and local feed mixers have been encouraged to carry them. Demand for these products is stimulated through an extension education campaign directed to the local farmers' groups.

Feed Components of the Project

The components of the feed package designed to make the raising of pigs commercially viable for small-scale farmers consisted of three elements: molasses, high-protein concentrate and ramie. The formula was developed in the late 1970s by the International Center for Tropical Agriculture in Palmira, Colombia, and in the School of Tropical Agriculture in Vera Cruz, Mexico.

Molasses. Molasses was included as a basic input in the swine feed formula for three reasons. First, it was an excellent source of energy. Second, it was produced domestically as a byproduct of sugar. Third, at the time the project was designed, it was inexpensive, because government subsidies made molasses the cheapest feed ingredient available in the Dominican Republic. Only distribution was thought to be a problem, because molasses was sold in bulk by the national sugar industry to large-scale users. CIMPA resolved the distribution issue by collaborating with three provincial development groups. It provided them with long-term loans of up RDP33,000, so that they could acquire large 2,000-gal. tanks for storing molasses purchased directly from industrial producers. From these tanks, the molasses could be transported to rural distribution points and sold to individual farmers.

Protein. The inclusion of a 40 percent protein supplement in the feed formula was essential to provide additional protein, minerals and vitamins lacking in the complete on-farm mix. It also increased total ration efficiency by supplementing the home-grown components and balancing the amino acid intake of the pigs.

Ramie. Ramie was selected as a feed input on the assumption that it could be grown despite local climatic variations to provide a year-round green fodder. Alternative sources of protein, such as sweet potato leaves and cassava tops, are as nutritious as ramie but are byproducts of seasonal cropping operations and therefore are available only during harvest periods. It was expected that the project could provide 2,000 campesinos (small farmers) enough rhizomes of ramie to plant one acre each by the end of 1985. This would have been sufficient to enable small-scale swine producers to meet annual shortfalls in traditional green fodder supplies.

Distribution Components of the Project

To get molasses and the protein supplement into the hands of rural farmers, CIMPA collaborated with three provincial development associations, each with a proved track record of providing extension services to rural farmers.

Campesinos Federados de Salcedo (CAFESA). Established a decade ago (1978), CAFESA is today one of the largest and most active multiservice cooperatives in Salcedo Province. It is composed of 136 groups and farmer associations. It has sponsored a wide range of community development projects, including both agricultural and livestock programs. Following the swine fever epidemic, CAFESA joined with Heifer Project International to establish one of the Dominican Republic's most effective swine multiplication and distribution programs. Many of the farmers participating in the ATI/CIMPA Project actually received their pigs through the CAFESA program.

One of CAFESA's most successful activities has been its community-based network of local retail outlets. Consisting of several storage and distribution centers, the network has enabled the federation to provide its membership with basic food and domestic supplies at the lowest prices possible. When CAFESA joined the Swine Feed Project in 1985, it decided to distribute molasses and the protein supplement through this retail network.

CAFESA was provided a loan of RDP20,000, which it used to purchase commercial feed inputs and the equipment needed to mill, mix, pack, transport and store them (bags, drums, tanks and so forth). They also undertook extension activities to introduce farmers to the project's feed formula. They wrote and distributed brochures instructing farmers how to prepare farm-based feed mixes. With a small fleet of trucks they were able to transport the prepared feeds to the retail outlets for purchase by local farmers (at no additional cost to the farmers).

Asociación para el Desarrollo de la Provincia Espaillat (ADEPE). ADEPE was founded in 1975 as a private, nonprofit organization devoted to the "socio-economic development and well-being of the inhabitants of Espaillat Province." ADEPE is involved with twenty farmer associations. Using more than US$2.5 million in financial assistance provided by the U.S. Agency for International Development (USAID), the International Bank for Reconstruction and Development (IBRD) and a variety of other national and international donor agencies, ADEPE has sponsored a wide range of agricultural, livestock and microenterprise programs.

Although ADEPE purchases, mills, mixes and packs feed ingredients at its own processing facilities, as does CAFESA, it has no retail outlets or any sizable fleet of transport vehicles for distribution. Instead, the independent farmer associations must purchase feed directly from ADEPE's feed processing center (GRAMA) and transport it at their own expense to their communities. However, ADEPE distinguished itself from CAFESA because it made available what amounts to short-term interest-free loans to each feed purchaser. Under the arrangement worked out by ADEPE, each association places an order with GRAMA for a specified amount of feed. The feed is then transported to the base community where it is deposited at a preassigned distribution point. In theory, the members of each group must pay for the feed they receive before they can place another order. In practice, however, GRAMA has been lenient in enforcing this condition of sale. The benefits of these variable short-term loans are obvious. They reduce production costs significantly because farmers are always, even after only one month, paying in devalued pesos (the annual currency devaluation vs. the US dollar is about 55 percent).

Federación Campesina Zambrana Chacuey. This foundation was founded in 1974 as a community-based action group. Today it includes 65 farmers' cooperatives, women's clubs and youth leagues throughout the province of Sanchez Ramirez. Membership is estimated to be between 2,000 and 4,000 people.

The Federación joined the project in July 1985 with a loan of RDP10,175 from CIMPA. The Federación purchases inputs on the open market in Santiago and transports them to its headquarters in Cotui. It has neither processing equipment nor a distribution network. The feed is sold at a profit of about RDP$1/hundredweight (cwt) to representatives of four member associations who, at their own expense, transport it to their respective base communities where it can be purchased locally by individual farmers. A markup of RDP1/cwt or roughly 3.5 percent of total sales has enabled the Federación to operate on a self-sustaining basis.

For many farmers, however, collaboration with CAFESA, ADEPE or the Federación was not a viable option. ADEPE's project loan fund was inadequate to support any more than the eleven associations currently participating in its program. In other cases, geographic isolation prevented the farmers from participating in a feed distribution network. For these reasons, CIMPA began providing loan funds directly to independent farmer groups. These intermediary groups assumed responsibility for distributing feed inputs, provided extension services and, where appropriate, managed loan funds.

Other Components of the Improved Technology Package

Extension workers instructed farmers in improved swine husbandry techniques; these included use of medicines and other veterinary products necessary for good health and construction of simple equipment such as farrowing crates, feed troughs and improved pig pens. CIMPA provided credit to farm cooperatives to finance the purchase of feed supplies in bulk; the cooperatives made small quantities of feed (generally a two-bag limit) available to farmers on credit.

Operation of Long-Term Credit Funds

In 1985, CIMPA provided RDP180,000 in non-interest bearing loans to three PDAs to establish separate long-term credit funds. The PDAs used these funds to provide loans to farmers groups to buy molasses handling and storage equipment. Loan terms were as long as three years at prevailing interest rates and were to be amortized over the last two and a half years of the loan period; the equipment and machinery served as the collateral for the loans. The PDAs were expected to treat the credit obligations of the farmers groups and the vendors as legally binding and to institute formal collection procedures when loans became delinquent.

Education and Technical Assistance Operations

To test the efficacy of the project's feed formula, demonstration units were established by CIMPA and CENIP. The two units were to establish ration standards, provide baseline data on feed conversion ratios, assess the nutritional value of the new feed formula and calculate savings and commercial feed substitutes. In addition to the feeding trials, CENIP was to carry out spot inspections of the high-protein concentrate being sold by authorized vendors. CENIP also was to check molasses for solids content, to avoid watering of the product. Two extension educators worked directly with participating vendors and farmer associations to demonstrate how the reference inputs could be incorporated into least cost/most efficient rations.

A Subsistence Activity Commercialized

The project opened the marketplace for small-scale swine producers. A subsistence activity has become a commercial activity. The change has had both positive and negative impacts. The cash income of the farmers has increased, and they have a chance of profiting from higher prices for their produce if demand increases. In other words, they might now benefit from the magic of the marketplace. Unfortunately, however, farmers now also stand to lose if prices fall. The following paragraphs describe a number of the positive impacts, as well as the negative ones, resulting from the project.

Positive Impact of the Project

In spite of increases in the cost of molasses, one of the important feed ingredients, farmers continued to report savings in cost and time. The establishment of local sales outlets saved farmers between RDP4 and RDP16 per quintile in transport costs. In addition, the availability of credit, which enabled farmers to purchase and stock feed for short periods, reduced demands on their time, as they no longer had to go to market several times a week.

To obtain an impression of the project's impact from the farmers' perspective, a non-representative survey was conducted among a sample of fifty independent farmers.[12] These results, independently verified in later interviews, provide the following picture: Farmers reported cost savings of about RDP57 per pig as a result of using the project's feed formula. Because a farmer sold an average of three and a half pigs in 1987, estimates are that each participating farmer who adopted the project's mixed feed ration increased average annual household income by approximately 18 percent (RDP200) over 1984 levels. This extra income has enabled some farmers to educate their children, buy additional property and improve their homes.

CIMPA estimates that approximately 2,600 farmers benefited from the project—a significant increase over the target number of 2,000. These farmers were able to make the transition to the formal sector and are now raising pigs as a commercial, profit-making venture.

The distribution of feed inputs, including molasses in the first year of the project, was a success. Loans given to associations to set up distribution outlets have been paid back in full with interest. More than 248 sales outlets were established using these loan funds. At least another 100 outlets have been established since then, bringing to 348 the total number of distribution outlets established between 1984 and 1988.

Higher turnover of inventory (feed) in association feed outlets has made it possible for the associations to charge lower prices, yet make higher than expected overall profits. Originally, it was estimated that feed would need to be marked up 15 percent to cover the added administrative and other associated costs. Because of the higher than expected inventory turnover, associations can charge markups of only 2-3 percent and still earn healthy profits. Farmers, through the associations, have access to low-cost feed that they otherwise would have been unable to obtain at any price.

The distribution scheme proved so successful that the government of Haiti asked USAID to assist it with another similar project. The technical director of the project in the Dominican Republic became the project director in Haiti.

Cuttings of ramie from the Dominican Republic were taken to Haiti to plant and grow under irrigation.

Negative Impact of the Project

By opening up the marketplace, farmers benefit, but they are also exposed to the price fluctuations that can occur in the market. A dramatic example of such a negative impact happened at the time the authors collected material for this study. In June 1988, the peso was devalued against the U.S. dollar from RDP6.80 to RDP8.20.[13] The devaluation resulted in an immediate increase in the cost of production, yet the sales price for pigs remained controlled by the government at RDP425 for a 100-kg pig. The new price to produce a 100-kg pig had gone up to RDP399, without taking the cost of labor into account. As a result, all farmers—large and small—tried to sell their pigs at once. The government, under pressure from the large-scale producers, agreed to purchase pigs from APORLI, COONA-PROCE and APORCI at the subsidized rate of RDP4 per kilogram. The agreement stipulated that the ministry would purchase twenty-five pigs per day from each producer. The pigs were to be transported to the Plazas Populares and more remote areas, where they would be sold for RDP5.50 per kilogram.[14]

In the project area, two slaughter and sales points were established. Two hundred and fifty pigs per week were sold in Licey, and up to one hundred pigs per week were sold in Puerto Plata. Although government intervention enabled medium- and large-scale producers to avoid losing money, small-scale producers were left to fend for themselves.

To understand the impact of the June 1988 crisis, it is necessary to divide small-scale farmers into two groups: those who belonged to an association (there are twenty associations in the Central Cibao Region), and those who did not.

Asociación de Cafeculturos de Moquita (ACM). The ACM is located in the mountains near Licey. Founded in 1981 and supported by CIMPA, it now has eighteen members who raise hogs in addition to coffee. CIMPA loaned RDP8,000 to the ACM to finance the feed distribution system. The ACM buys its feed from Alimentos Balanceados. As described previously, the ACM delivers the feed and provides small credit to its members.

The ACM established a distribution point where feed and veterinary supplies sold at a markup of RDP1 per quintile (100 lbs.). Occasionally, feed is sold to outsiders recommended by association members. The ACM maintains relations with middlemen in Licey, Moca and Santiago who regularly visit the villages to purchase the mature pigs.

Because the ACM was able to stay informed of market and currency changes, most of its members could sell off their pigs immediately following the devaluation of the peso. Working together, the farmers transported their pigs to markets in the towns of Licey, Moca and Santiago. The pigs were sold for RDP3 per kilogram for older stock (sows) and RDP3.5 per kilogram for young stock. Average holdings per ACM member dropped from eleven pigs in

1987 to three pigs by the end of June 1988.

Corazón de Maria. In Guayabilla, some 15 km from the town of Moca, are two associations that CIMPA has supported over the years. A multipurpose men's association, La Progresista, purchases agricultural inputs, markets produce (especially coffee) and operates a savings and credit society. Most of the wives of the members of La Progresista belong to Corazón de Maria (Heart of Maria) a women's association devoted entirely to swine production. Corazón de Maria is part of the Federación de Campesinos and receives loans, technical assistance and water from the Federación Equipos Sociales y Agrarios (FESA).

Corazón de Maria has an outlet for swine feed, veterinary supplies and vegetables. Only members can buy on credit; all others must pay cash at the time of sale. The association purchases feed from the cooperative in Moca and transports it by truck to Guayabilla. Most of the feed, like cassava, bananas, beans and potatoes, is cultivated by the members.

Because many members of Corazón de Maria have husbands and other family who are active in La Progresista and FESA, the women learned about the devaluation almost as soon as it was announced. They were able to arrange transport to a market, where their excess stock was sold. Mature (95–100 kg) pigs were sold for RDP3 per kilogram; immature pigs and piglets were sold for much less. After the devaluation, average pig holdings per association member dropped by more than 50 percent. Most of the pigs that the women kept were either pregnant or lactating.

Individual Farmers

The effects of the June 1988 devaluation of the peso were far more severe for the small farmers who did not belong to farmers' associations and thus were not immediately aware of its consequences. Because these farmers lacked information and access to transport, they found it far more difficult to sell their excess stock. As a result, they were left with many more pigs to feed. Because they had to purchase feed from retail outlets at a greatly increased price, most of their potential profits were consumed by feed costs. Overall, small independent farmers are far more vulnerable to cyclical changes in the price of pork and feed than are farmers who belong to the associations.

Although some farmers wish to remain independent, most of those interviewed expressed a desire to join an association. Unfortunately, geographic isolation, lack of communication or lack of time prevent some farmers from participating in an association.

Lesson Learned: The Need for Cooperation

The project has demonstrated the positive impact small market-oriented interventions can have. It also demonstrated how the vulnerability of farmers can increase. One of the important lessons that farmers learned in this transition from subsistence to commercial farming is the importance of cooperation and effective organization. Only by working together were farmers able to shield themselves from the disastrous effects of the June 1988 devaluation. Because the farmers were organized, they were able to receive assistance from CIMPA, FESA and international agencies such as ATI. Furthermore, by organizing, many farmers could, for the first time, obtain a loan from a commercial bank. As members of an organized production unit, they learned about the feed component, the equipment needed to process it and the realities of their new position in the market.

Notes

1. *World Development Report 1988* (Oxford: Oxford University Press, 1988).
2. *World Development Report 1988,* p. 365.
3. In 1979 the external debt was 31.5 percent of GDP; in 1983 it had already risen to 55.2 percent (Central Bank and IMF Statistics, in *World Development Report 1988,* p. 370).
4. Christopher Story, *The Latin American Times* 7 (8), (London, 1986), p. 3.
5. *International Financial Statistics* (IFS) 41 (1) (Washington, D.C.: 1988), p. 189.
6. By this time, 21,600 gallons of molasses had been distributed.
7. This is the current market price. Most farmers, however, raise their own piglets. In those cases, the cost involves feed for the female pig during gestation and lactation, slightly less than the market price.
8. Jose Luis Rojas, "Commercial-Economic Evaluation: Swine Feed Delivery System for Small Farmers," *Evaluation Report* (Santiago: Appropriate Technology International, 1987), p. 5.
9. The price for pig pens and handling equipment is based on a material cost of RDP100 over a five-year period.
10. Carl Liedholm and Donald C. Mead, "Small-Scale Enterprises in Developing Countries: Empirical Evidence and Policy Implications," MSU International Development Papers No. 9, Michigan State University, 1987; Albert Berry, Mariluz Cortes, and Ashfaq Ishaq, "On the Dynamism of Small and Medium Industry in Colombia: Some Possible Lessons," in Frances Stewart, Henk Thomas and Ton de Wilde, *The Other Policy* (London: IT Publications, 1990).
11. Christian Strutz, "Technical Assessment: Swine Feed Delivery System for Small Farmers" in *Evaluation Report* (Santiago: Appropriate Technology International, 1987), p. 4.
12. Lack of baseline data made it impossible to measure precisely the extent to which the project increased farmers income.
13. *International Financial Statistics* 41(1) (1988).
14. Pork prices are cyclical over a three- to five-year period and do fluctuate in response to supply and demand, even though the government regulates consumer prices. At the time the authors visited the Dominican Republic in June 1988, pork prices were at a low point in the cycle. By September 1989, prices had swung back up and were high in comparison to the cost of production (RDP12.00/kg for meat versus RDP6.75/kg for the cost of production). As a result of the higher production price, small-scale producers in the country are retaining large numbers of female pigs to breed.

7 Providing Poor *Tambak* Farms in Indonesia Access to a Lucrative Market

PAK PARTI lives with his wife, a six-year-old son and a two-month-old daughter in a small fishing village off the main road to Bakarin on the island of Java. Pak Parti's relatives, and those of his wife, live nearby, as is customary in this country. Pak Parti and his father-in-law own a one-hectare (ha) brackish water pond called a *tambak*; they share the income derived from the pond equally. During the dry season, they collect salt from the pond, which is quite profitable. In the rainy season, they raise milkfish. The *tambak* provides a stable, albeit moderate, income.

Because income from the *tambak* is not sufficient to support two families, Pak Parti works as a day laborer for other pond owners and for the Yayasan Dian Desa (YDD) Outgrowers Shrimp Company, which is promoting intensified shrimp production. Pak Parti wanted to reap the rewards of the more lucrative shrimp production, but he and his father-in-law did not believe they could afford to miss a milkfish harvest while they waited for their pond to be improved. So, instead of joining the YDD partnership program, they decided to try shrimp production on their own. They did not improve their pond, nor did they receive any technical assistance—two services that would have been provided by the program.

After Pak Umbar, another *tambak* farmer, reported two excellent harvests as a result of joining YDD's Outgrowers Program, Pak Parti and his father-in-law agreed to participate. Now they are waiting for their pond to be improved so that it can be stocked with juvenile shrimp. Pak Parti hopes he and his father-in-law will be as successful as Pak Umbar. If his dreams come true, soon he will be earning five times as much annually from shrimp production as he did from milkfish and salt cultivation. Then, "All my money troubles will be over," he muses.

Driven by a weight- and health-conscious public and increasing per capita incomes, the world market for tiger prawns (large shrimp) is strong and growing, especially in the industrialized countries of Europe, the United States and Japan. The U.S. and European markets are supplied almost exclusively by Central and South America. Japan imports shrimp from Asia, notably Taiwan, Indonesia, the Philippines, India and Bangladesh. (See Table 7-1.)

Table 7-1   Sales of Whole Shrimps to the Japanese Market
(in thousand metric tons), 1980–84

Year	Domestic Landings	Imports	Total Supply
1980	51	143	194
1981	55	162	217
1982	60	151	211
1983	64	149	211
1984	62	169	231
Annual Growth Rate (%)	5.0	4.3	4.5

Source: World Bank Report (Washington, D.C., 1986) in *Project Plan for the Implementation of the Hatchery and Outgrowers Service Unit* (Yogyakarta: Yayasan Dian Desa, Mimeograph, 1987), p. 8.

These five Asian countries produce 80 percent of Asia's pond-cultured shrimp, and their production is escalating. The availability of brackish water ponds and new technologies that can dramatically increase the low productivity of current shrimp production promise large increases in yield in the future.

In all five Asian countries, heavy investments are being made in establishing or upgrading shrimp production. In 1988, nine out of ten applications to the International Finance Corporation (IFC) regional office in Bangkok were requests for loans to invest in shrimp production. Although competition is increasing, world market analysis shows that, over the next ten years, demand is expected to grow faster than supply—even using conservative estimates for shrimp consumption and optimistic estimates for increased production capacity.[1]

Tambak Aquaculture in Indonesia: An Introduction

Indonesia's large areas of brackish coastal waters and its cheap labor supply give it a natural and economic advantage over other shrimp-producing countries. Although lack of soil fertility makes the coastal land areas of many of Indonesia's 13,700 islands unsuitable for agriculture, these areas are well suited to fish and shrimp cultivation. At present, these coastal areas are used for salt mining and traditional forms of aquaculture, carried out in *tambaks*— brackish water ponds.

In an effort to diversify Indonesia's economy to offset the declining income from oil resources, the government of Indonesia decided to stimulate shrimp production. Table 7-2, which compares the Third and Fourth Five-Year Plans for the fisheries sector, demonstrates the significant shift in resources. The budget for the Fourth Five-Year Plan is more than five times the amount allocated in the previous Five-Year Plan. Even without the massive influx of government resources projected in the Fourth Five-Year Plan, shrimp production has increased dramatically, as shown in Table 7-3.

Table 7-2   Fisheries Development Budget in the Third Five-Year Plan (1978–83), and Projected Budget for the Fourth Five-Year Plan (1984–89), (in millions of Rupiah).

Sources	Third Five-Year Plan	Fourth Five-Year Plan	Growth Rate (%)
Central development budget	62,322	520,560	735%
Routine budget	10,913	65,600	501
Regional development budget	18,330	128,500	601
Bank credits	76,233	1,392,189	1,726
Foreign aid	299,000[a]	583,891	95
Capital investment	74,803[b]	236,777	216
Domestic	10,322	200,111	1,838
Foreign	64,481	36,666	–43
Total	541,601	2,927,517	441%

Source: Wolfgang Hannig, *Towards a Blue Revolution: A Study on Socioeconomic Aspects of Brackish Waterpond Cultivation in Java* (Yogyakarta: Yayasan Dian Desa, 1988), p. 61.
[a] Converted into Indonesian Rupiah on the basis of US$1 = IndRp1,000.
[b] This figure covers the period from 1969–70.

Traditional aquaculture takes place in *tambaks* where either only milkfish (monoculture) or milkfish and shrimp (polyculture) are cultivated. More than 20,000 hectares (ha) of the over 180,000 ha of coastal areas used for *tambaks* in Indonesia in 1985 were located in central Java. Most of these *tambaks* were in the northern part of the island, where the soil composition (40 percent clay, 40 percent sand and 20 percent silt) is favorable. *Tambak* farming is a typical small-holder activity. Most *tambaks* (more than 98 percent) are 1 ha or less.

The People of Tambak Aquaculture[2]

The people involved in *tambak* aquaculture can be divided into four groups: owners, tenants, fish pond laborers and traders. In the current social system in

Indonesia, only men can be owners and tenants. Laborers are mostly men, but occasionally women are allowed. Women are active as traders of shrimp and fish.

Table 7-3   Shrimp Production in 1976 and 1982 (in metric tons)

Sector	1976		1982	
Tambak cultivation	14,621	(11%)	31,082	(21%)
Inland open fisheries	5,910	(4%)	11,313	(7%)
Marine fisheries	113,051	(85%)	108,499	(72%)
Total production	133,582	(100%)	150,894	(100%)

Source: Wolfgang Hannig, *Towards a Blue Revolution: Study on Socioeconomic Aspects of Brackish Waterpond Cultivation in Java,* Yogyakarta (Yayasan Dian Desa, 1988), p. 51.

Owners. Some owners work directly in the pond assisted by the laborers. Others do not work the ponds themselves, but rent them to tenants.

Tenants. Tenants do not own ponds but work in ponds owned by others. A tenant may rent the pond and pay a predetermined rent to the pond owner for a specific period, or participate in a *sakap* or 50-50 sharing of the product,[3] a system similar to sharecropping. The regulations for the sharing arrangements vary from pond to pond. Terms are often influenced by the type of family ties and personal relations existing between the tenant and the owner.

Fish Pond Laborers. Pond laborers work and receive compensation in cash or in kind (pond produce). Laborers are divided into two groups: permanent and part-time. The permanent laborer takes care of the ponds on behalf of the owners or tenants. He or she operates the gates to let the tide come in, catches the shrimp and fish that are accidentally caught in the pond and guards the pond. Generally, permanent laborers are paid monthly, either in cash or in kind or by a combination of the two. But because of the different forms of the relationships among the owner, tenant and laborer, many remuneration systems exist.

Pay of part-time laborers is generally based on time worked and type of work performed. For example, for pond improvements (digging, moving of earth and so forth), a laborer who works from 8:00 a.m. to 4:00 p.m., with a two-hour rest at noontime, earns 1,500 Indonesian Rupiahs (approximately US$1).[4] During the harvest season, when labor is in high demand and specific skills are required, a part-time laborer can be paid as much as IndRp2,500/day.

Traders. Many traders earn their livelihood from traditional *tambak* farming. Traders generally fit into one of three categories: trader farmers, semi-independent middlemen (or women) and small-time middlemen.

Trader farmers form an association or corporation. They combine their production and buy additional shrimp from nonmembers who bring their produce to the collection site. One of the members of the association transports the produce to the cold storage facility in the city. An example of such an association is Ngraci, a village north of Semarang. Ngraci's collection center/marketplace is on the main road to Bakarin. One of the members owns a car that is used to transport the produce daily to the nearest cold storage in Bakarin, or to the seaport of Semarang, 80 km away. Transport charges per farmer are IndRp5,000 to Bakarin and IndRp35,000 to Semarang.

Semi-independent middlemen or women act on behalf of the owners of cold storage facilities in the larger towns. In order to keep their warehouses filled, the owners of the cold storage facilities lend the semi-independent middlemen money to buy the shrimp, which they purchase from small-time middlemen and from the farmers. The loan stipulates that the shrimp can be sold only to the warehouse owners. As a result, the competitive position of the semi-independent middlemen is limited compared to truly independent middlemen, who can sell purchased produce to the warehouse owner paying the highest price.

Both semi-independent and independent middlemen also establish ties with breeders and tenants. Before the harvest, these middlemen will lend breeders and tenants cash provided they sell their shrimp back to the middlemen at prearranged prices, almost always a price less than the going market rate.

Finally, there are the small-time middlemen, or in this case, nearly exclusively middlewomen, known in the Bahasan Indonesian language as "the person accepting payment in advance." These traders go to the ponds every morning and afternoon to buy the shrimp or fish and then sell them to the semi-independent and independent traders. Small-time middlemen borrow the money for their trade in advance from the independent and semi-independent traders; in return they must sell the shrimp they buy to the trader/person from whom they borrowed the money. Thus, they also are known as "the hands and feet of the big trader."

The Traditional Shrimp and Fish Production Process

Traditional farmers involved in pond cultivation (men) own an average of 1 ha of land, which they use to cultivate any one or a combination of milkfish, accidentally caught or stocked shrimp and salt. In some areas, like the north-east portion of central Java, traditional aquaculture usually combines the milkfish and salt production. During the dry season, the farmers collect the salt left in the middle of the pond, which is surrounded by a channel used to breed fish. During the rainy season, farmers stock the channel with milkfish or a combination of milkfish and shrimp. Salt production requires minimal labor and equipment, except for harvesting/collection. Salt is contained in the seawater; when the water evaporates, the salt that is left can be collected and sold. Income earned by salt collection is higher per ha than that from milkfish or shrimp—IndRp1,000,000 per ha for salt vs. IndRp500,000 per ha for milkfish or shrimp. However, salt can be collected only a few months out of the year (August–October). A pond owner cannot subsist on salt collection alone, although most small- and medium-size *tambak* owners report that about 50 percent of their income results from the sale of salt.

Monoculture Production

Most *tambak* farmers cultivate only milkfish (a monoculture) and some accidentally caught shrimp. This traditional form of aquaculture is familiar and easy, and presents few risks. Traditional pond management involves the following:[5]

- Preparation stage: After milkfish, or *bandeng,* are harvested, the ponds are dried for one to two weeks. Natural medicine (antiseptic roots) or chemicals (thiodin) are added to destroy possible diseases. At this time, water gates and dikes may be repaired or improved, the pond deepened, and a section of the pond is set aside for a nursery. Most of the time manure is scattered on the bottom of the pond to create algae upon which the fish will feed.
- Scattering of *bibit* (baby fish): Before the *bibit* are distributed throughout the pond, they are scattered in the nursery section, where they mature during the next fifteen to twenty days. The nursery stay also enables the *bibit* to adapt to the conditions in the pond.
- Although most traditional farmers rely on the tide to bring in *bibit*, some farmers purchase additional *bibit.* More practical *tambak* owners buy small fish—*glondongan*—which need to remain in the nursery for only two days before beginning their rapid growth. Purchasing *glondongan* is more expensive than purchasing *bibit,* but the risk of failure is reduced.
- Breeding stage: After the *bibit/glondongan* are transferred to the main pond area to begin their growth, the only major chore involves changing the water during high tide. Algae and plankton in the pond provide food for the milkfish.

Traditional monoculture involves few risks but produces little income. Almost no capital or labor is required prior to harvest. Farmers rely on the tide to bring in the fish stock, which may be supplemented by purchased *bibit* or *glondongan.* The majority of the *tambak* owners cultivate only milkfish, which is not a high-value product. Even with a biannual harvest, income from the pond is low. Average production of milkfish ranges from 50 to 200 kg per ha per season. Market price per kilo is IndRp1,500. Thus two harvests bring an average income per ha of IndRp150,000–600,000 per year (US$100–$375). As most *tambak* farmers own only one ha of pond, this is their total yearly cash income. Tenants, who have to pay rent or pay the owner a share of the production, net even less.

Most farmers supplement their income from the sale of milkfish by selling the small wild shrimp and other fish that the tide carries into their ponds. They gather wild shrimp, usually at night, in a net they place at the water gate or other strategic area. Additional income from this harvest averages IndRp4,000 making an estimated additional income of IndRp100,000 (US$59) a year. Thus, a family of four persons has to live on an average yearly income of US$312, an amount much lower than the average gross national product (GNP) per capita in Indonesia of US$490.[6]

Polyculture Production

In a polyculture operation, the farmer stocks both milkfish and shrimp fry. Farmers who maintain a polyculture might earn a bit more than those who maintain a monoculture, but this method also requires more investment, labor, time and thus more risk. Because the tide brings in only a few shrimp fry, the farmer has to buy fry from the nearest hatchery, which is usually quite a distance from his *tambak*. Or he may purchase fry at a higher price from small-scale traders who come to the ponds.

Farmers who maintain traditional low-density ponds (where the milkfish/fry population is less than three to ten thousand per ha) can rely on the algae and plankton in the pond to serve as feed. Farmers who increase the density of fish and shrimp in their ponds must supplement the natural feed. They can drop manure into the ponds to stimulate the growth of more algae and plankton and/or purchase feed, is the most expensive cost component of aquaculture. Traditional ponds in which the farmer has attempted to stock fish and shrimp at higher than natural density, report low survival rates.

Negative Effects of a Strong Market Demand and Early Government Schemes

Government schemes that encouraged investments in shrimp production initially were limited to owners of two-ha ponds or larger.[7] As 98 percent of *tambak* farmers own ponds smaller than two ha, they were not eligible to participate in the early schemes. Worse yet, the small holders found it even more difficult to compete against the government-subsidized small group of large landowners.

The government's program had other negative effects on small owners and tenants. Higher net returns caused the price of the *tambaks* to escalate rapidly; tenants were confronted by higher rents and tougher sharecropping conditions. The landowner/tenant agreements were no longer based on actual returns but on projected pond potential. Small sharecroppers who could not live on lower returns or obtain the resources to intensify production, such as part-time laborers, were the first casualties.

Small-pond owners are also in a precarious position. Although they have not been forced to sell their lands or to intensify production, they are very much aware of their low yields and poor profits. Nonetheless, because of increased demand, their land has rapidly appreciated in value. Small *tambak* farmers are offered IndRp10,000,000 per ha for their ponds (US$5,434), which is approximately twelve times their annual income. The large amount of money is tempting and many small *tambak* farmers have sold their land, despite the fact that this land was their only source of regular income.

Other farmers have tried to keep their land and increase its productivity.

The potential is promising. Traditional farmers have an average income of US$312; this is based on earnings of IndRp400,000 per year (US$250) from raising milkfish and some additional income from selling the shrimp and other fish they catch at the gates of their ponds. This amount contrasts sharply with their anticipated income from intensified shrimp production. On two shrimp harvests per year, *tambak* farmers can earn as much as IndRp2,880,000 or US$1,700 annually—more than five times their current income.

Thus, the small holder is faced with a difficult choice. He can sell his pond for what to him is a very large sum of money and lose his regular source of income, or he can improve his pond's productivity. To switch to intensified shrimp production, he needs to improve his pond physically and stock it with shrimp fry; these requirements demand working capital, which he does not have. He also needs the technical knowledge to undertake the new type of aquaculture.

The Promises of Intensified Small-Scale Shrimp Production and Marketing

In 1984, the government of Indonesia launched Intam, a program to increase shrimp production that included small holders—the 98 percent of *tambak* farmers who own less than two ha of land. From a technical perspective, it is a mystery why the government excluded the small-scale *tambak* farmers from earlier schemes. It can be argued that their exclusion was based on a mistaken belief about economies of scale—mistaken because shrimp production is a technology that, if all factors are taken into account, is basically scale neutral.

Intensified Shrimp Production: A Scale-Neutral Technology

The discussion of economies of scale goes back to the nineteenth century, when fixed and indirect costs of production first emerged as important elements of economic theory. A detailed study on this subject is given in Pratten,[8] who defined economies of scale as "reductions in average costs attributable to increases in scale." Thus, in the case of shrimp production, the larger the pond area under cultivation, the lower the cost to operate the pond, which would result in a lower production price per shrimp.

Any business—and shrimp production is no exception—involves fixed and variable costs. The fixed costs of shrimp production include the cost of the land the improvements made to the land, investments in pumps and aerators and, because of the specialized nature of shrimp production, the cost of management. The variable costs include the fry, food, medical supplies, labor, marketing and distribution costs.

There are two possible ways to increase the size of operations. If the larger farm still uses one-ha ponds as the unit of operation, the only source of economies of scale would be associated with the size of the firm—such as volume purchases of inputs and more efficient marketing. If the size of the pond is increased beyond one ha, there may also be economies of scale from a larger operation as well. The fixed costs of the pumps and aerators and the unit costs of land improvements may be reduced.

These advantages may be offset by increased risks. The greater the number of shrimp that are contained in one unit, the greater the number of shrimp that will die if a disease breaks out. Disease is not an isolated, infrequent event. In fact, the average survival rate of shrimp 21 days after their larval state is only 20–30 percent.

The reduction in costs made possible by larger size operating units is offset either by higher losses or by additional costs for medicines to keep the shrimp alive. All variable costs directly relate to the number of shrimp produced. Thus, the only advantage of larger units is a lower distribution cost, which on the highly populated island of Java, with a relatively well-developed infrastructure, does not provide much of a competitive edge.

The Intam Credit Scheme

Intam, the credit scheme launched by the government of Indonesia in 1984 to improve the productivity of aquaculture, was the first such program that did not exclude farmers who owned less than two ha of land. Unfortunately, very few small-scale *tambak* farmers have taken advantage of Intam, for reasons that will be described below.[9]

In general, small farmers rarely obtain official bank loans; the banks are reluctant to grant such small loans and the farmers do not want and are too poor to apply for official large loans. Thus, at first, Intam appeared quite promising. Special attention was directed to farmers who cultivated between .10 ha and less than two ha. Tenants, as well as owners, could qualify for credit —provided the tenants had entered into a formal tenancy arrangement.

Intam offers four credit packages; they range from IndRp1,214,000 for low density monoculture to IndRp3,380,000 to engage in dual density polyculture.[10] Although the amount of credit to which these small farmers are given access is high, the repayment period for capital investments is eight years, whereas working capital loans need to be repaid in five years. The annual interest rate averages 12 percent.

Intam borrowers need to meet the following conditions:

* The borrower must be a resident of the area where the pond is situated; that is, absentee landowners do not qualify.
* The borrower has to be willing and able to apply new technology and production methods as suggested by the fisheries extension officer and other officials from the District Fisheries Service.
* The borrower has to be experienced in *tambak* management.
* The borrower has to be willing to cooperate with the *tambak* peasant group where his pond is located. The peasant group is a non-governmental but government-controlled group, working at village or village cluster level (ten to twenty persons).

- The borrower may sell his shrimp harvest more or less at will, but must sell milkfish yields to the institutions recommended by the government-run cooperative at the village level.

Furthermore, before the application can be approved, the credit applicant has to obtain a *"Tambak* Land Certificate for Intam Participants" and an "Akte Credit Verband" (Credit Association Certificate). These certificates cost IndRp60,000 (US$36) each. Because the government anticipated that most of the targeted applicants would not have this amount of money, it allows the certificate fees to be prefinanced. The procedure for prefinancing, however, is fairly complicated and involves four parties. Obtaining the certificates is only one of a total of nineteen steps necessary to obtain the credit.[11] The process involves numerous government officials at different administrative levels.

Although in theory the Intam program provides an opportunity for small and medium cultivators to improve their productivity, few of the eligible farmers have taken advantage of the opportunity. Farmers do not apply for a loan from the Intam scheme for the following reasons:

- The Intam program is very bureaucratic; it might take eighteen months or longer to process the loan after the certificates are obtained. Small cultivators are usually reluctant to deal with bureaucracies and numerous government institutions.
- The certificates, a precondition to obtain Intam credits, cost IndRp60,000 each. Not only does this step require additional bureaucratic red tape, but the peasants must pay the IndRp60,000 before their loan is approved. It is common knowledge that it also creates another opportunity for officials to demand the notorious *uang kopi* (literally coffee money, but actually a bribe) for services.
- Even the smallest loan offered by the scheme is still far too large for the average *tambak* farmer. Repayment of principal and interest far exceed his current income. Thus if the improvements he can make with the loan do not lead to a substantially higher income, the *tambak* farmer will never be able to pay off his loan and the bank will take possession of his land. Few farmers are willing to take this risk.
- The amount of credit offered is astronomical for the target group. Fortunately, the small holders have not applied for these huge amounts of credit.

The fisheries extension officers have limited knowledge of technology and production methods; neither do they have time to explain the program to the farmers. Yet the extension officers issue directives, which the farmers must follow as a condition for the loan. This regulation is intended to ensure Intam's success. Unfortunately, even the private sector, which pays wages ten times those of the Government, cannot recruit qualified extension officers.

As a result, very few small *tambak* farmers have applied for a loan within the Intam system. They continue traditional aquaculture and borrow small amounts from local middlemen or family members to upgrade their operations gradually. When Intam was created in 1984–85, 11,300 ha had been scheduled for intensified aquaculture using Intam credits. As of 1988, only 42 ha or 0.37 percent of the original schedule had been intensified.[12] The Intam program has not been accepted by the targeted small and medium cultivators.

A Need for Technical Assistance and Innovative Financing: The YDD/Outgrowers Service Unit Scheme

The intricacies of intensified shrimp production cannot be transferred from father to son. Intensified production involves new technologies and new methods. The investment in terms of capital and learning time is too costly for small-scale *tambak* farmers. Government schemes, even those that were especially designed for the small-scale *tambak* farmer, did not work. Yayasan Dian Desa, a nonprofit private development organization, recognized that if traditional *tambaks* were to be converted from salt/fish production to intensified shrimp farming, farmers needed not only hands-on technical assistance but a risk-sharing mechanism to finance the necessary investments. Using the concept of a venture capital model, YDD, with Appropriate Technology International (ATI) assistance, decided to fill this market niche, which appeared to suit their mission and capabilities.

Organization of the Project

YDD is a nonprofit, nongovernmental community development organization established in 1972 to give people in rural areas access to appropriate technology, to better exploit their economic assets and to improve their income. YDD approaches development from the bottom up, emphasizing grassroots actions and use of field-tested technologies. The solutions feature the active participation of the proposed beneficiaries.

Early activities of YDD were directed to fulfilling the people's basic needs, especially providing drinking water. As the years passed, YDD learned that fulfilling basic needs did not automatically improve living standards. YDD began to focus on income-generating productive activities in agriculture, food technology, energy and small-scale industry.

Most of YDD's work was financed by domestic and foreign donations. As various activities began to yield returns and the organization continued to grow, YDD realized that it needed its own income-generating source within the context of a nonprofit organization. Thus, it began to look for an income-generating capacity that would not only have commercial promise, but also be socially relevant.

In 1983, with assistance from ATI, YDD established a venture capital company (VCC) to facilitate the creation of enterprises to benefit low-income people. The VCC was to accomplish several functions. First, it was to identify investment opportunities. Second, because low-income people have few assets and scarce financial resources, the VCC would organize the financing needed to take advantage of a new investment opportunity. Third, the VCC would undertake the initial organization and management until the fledgling enterprise became successful. Underlying all these plans was the assumption that the VCC would be competent to review investment opportunities in a wide variety of fields and to oversee the development and management of these diverse enterprises.

The VCC's early experiences convinced YDD that it is not realistic to expect a VCC to be able to analyze opportunities in a wide variety of fields. YDD decided to focus its attention on the field of shrimp production—a sector that had the potential to benefit low-income people and that could draw upon YDD's technical skills and proven approach to community-based enterprise development. YDD's considerable experience in shrimp production is summarized below.

In 1984, YDD assisted a local business group to manage its shrimp hatchery, Indra. Based on that experience and on a study of the people who bought the fry from the Indra hatchery, YDD decided to invest further in the shrimp-farming business.

YDD started a trial *tambak* research project. Two ha of ponds in the middle of traditional *tambak* farms were rented and managed by YDD staff. In addition to increasing YDD's technical expertise, this experiment provided knowledge about the social condition of the poor *tambak* farmers and the traditional sharecropping structure and marketing techniques.

In August 1986, YDD opened unit one of a planned two-unit hatchery at Jepara in north central Java. Unit Number One can produce about one million fry per month. The hatchery is the first component of an ATI/YDD project to upgrade traditional *tambak* farming. The Outgrowers Service Unit (OSU), the second component, is described in more detail below.

The Product: Tiger Prawns

YDD forms a partnership with the local *tambak* owners to produce tiger prawns. This variety of prawn was selected because of its marketability, rapid growth rate and ease of production. High demand for tiger prawns in foreign markets, notably in Japan, results in premium prices relative to other varieties of prawn. The tiger prawn is large; individuals from offshore catches often reach 500–600 grams in body weight. The species grows rapidly and can tolerate relatively large fluctuations in salinity and water temperature. Survival rates of up to 90 percent have been reported during the last two months of growth before the harvest.

Because of the premium prices paid by buyers in Japan, Indonesian tiger prawns are produced almost exclusively for export. Because they are usually eaten fresh, not frozen, product quality is especially important. Important quality attributes of the end product beside freshness include appearance, regularity of packing, assurance of portion control and cleanliness. The *tambak* farmer can improve the quality of the prawns in two ways: preventing damage during harvest and quickly delivering the tiger prawn to cold storage.

The project has two components, the Hatchery and the OSU. The latter consists of a nursery pond, a demonstration pond and extension services to help the *tambak* farmers produce and market the shrimp.

The Hatchery

The supply of fry in Indonesia has been declining for several years for the following reasons:[13]

- Overharvesting by large industrial shrimp trawlers;
- Pollution and destruction of mangrove forests, which devastate shrimp breeding grounds; and
- Cessation of operations at several large hatcheries.

YDD opened two hatcheries at the same time that others were closing—not because the demand for fry was falling, but because of huge losses resulting from poor management practices. Hatchery operation is a complex business that requires constant attention to quality of water, food, temperature and lighting. Additional parameters related to the physical characteristics of the tiger prawn need to be monitored at each stage of development. Many hatcheries have been unable to attract quality staff who have both technical skills and a sense of dedication and team spirit.

In the well-equipped hatcheries, the average industrial survival rate of fry from age PL1 to PL21 is approximately 8 percent. Many hatcheries could not even achieve this survival rate. YDD, both in the Indra hatchery and later in Hatchery Number One, reported average survival rates of more than 20 percent over periods of several months.

Hatchery Unit One, which can produce one million PLs every 26 days, provides a steady supply of high-quality fry to expand small holder production of shrimp. The hatchery sells PL21 both to independent shrimp farmers not participating in the project and to the OSC, which stocks them in its nursery pond. The OSU raises the PL21s in the nursery pond until as juveniles (PL60s) they can be sold to the participating *tambak* farmers who grow them to maturity.

The Outgrowers Service Unit

The Outgrowers Service Unit, the focal point of the project, forms partnerships with small pond owners to make their shrimp cultivation more profitable. The OSU consists of a nursery pond, demonstration ponds and the ongoing technical and management services provided participating pond owners. The pond owners provide their ponds and labor. In addition to supplying fry, feed, other inputs and ongoing technical and management assistance, the OSU provides the initial capital, labor and technical assistance necessary to upgrade the ponds for intensified shrimp production. The OSU also helps the farmers locate and secure markets for the harvested tiger prawns.

The Nursery Pond

Initially, farmers participating in the OSU Program received PL21s to raise to maturity. The early trial-and-error experiments, however, revealed that the survival rate in the farmers' ponds for PLs between age PL21 and PL60 was only 20-30 percent. Therefore, YDD decided to raise the PL21s in a special nursery until the fry become juveniles (PL60s). This procedure has substantially improved PL survival rates, which now average 80 percent in the nursery.

From the hatchery, PL21s are shipped to the OSU nursery pond, where they remain for one and a half to two months until they become juveniles. Water in the nursery pond is exchanged regularly by tidal flushing and/or pumping. Supplementary feeding consists of trash fish, mussels and so forth. Dried coconut leaves are usually floated on the pond to provide shade. The PL60s are then collected in a bag net installed at the drainage gate and transferred to the demonstration pond or the ponds of participating farmers.

The Demonstration Pond

A demonstration pond was established near the outgrowers' *tambaks*. In this pond, the OSU raises the juveniles until they are ready to be harvested. The demonstration pond:

- enables local *tambak* owners to see firsthand the improved pond management practices. Farmers are taught the importance of water quality and soil quality. They observe the careful procedures to check salinity, temperature, algae growth and density of shrimp, adjust the feed and control disease.
- serves as a marketing tool to attract farmers to join the YDD/OSU partnership program. Most farmers have seen other farmers attempt to intensify their production without the benefit of extension services—and fail. The demonstration pond shows the farmers what they will be undertaking—the risks and the pay-off.
- provides YDD with an opportunity to conduct research on improved shrimp production technologies in actual field settings. Better methods of aeration, various feed formulas and different salinity levels because of drought or heavy rainfall are among the many variables that need further research.
- provides income for the OSU. Sales of the fully grown tiger prawns raised in the demonstration pond supplement income from the hatchery and from the partnership sharing program.

Extension Services: Partnerships

The OSU enters into partnerships with individual pond owners. Even ponds as small as 0.75 ha may be owned by as many as eight or nine members of a family. Because all family members must agree to such a partnership, reaching agreement on the partnership is often not an easy task.

OSU staff are always available to discuss the partnership arrangements, as they remain in the area to monitor the nursery and demonstration ponds and to provide technical advice to farmers already participating in the OSU. In addition to technical and marketing extension services, the OSU provides all the required material inputs such as juvenile shrimp, feed, fertilizer and a share of the capital and labor needed for the pond improvements. Because participating farmers receive PL60s rather than PL21s, their risk is substantially reduced. Reducing the rearing time until maturity by forty days gives the farmers the opportunity to obtain at least one additional harvest.

The farmers provide the *tambak* and their labor and agree to participate in the partnership for at least six cycles (two years). YDD believes that this period is sufficient to permit the farmers to become skilled in intensified shrimp production. At the same time, the profits earned during the partnership should allow YDD to recover its initial investment, including the cost to improve the pond. After the first agreement concludes, farmers have two options: Enter a new partnership agreement with the OSU or become independent and obtain credit from banks or from government schemes, such as Intam.

The 50–50 sharing system in the project is a variation of the traditional sharing system, where the total catch is divided equally between tenant and landowner. The traditional system, however, requires few inputs. Intensified shrimp production requires improved ponds, additional fry, feed and—in instances of disease—medicines. After the OSU deducts the cost for the juveniles, feed, fertilizer and medicines, the profits are split 50–50 between the OSU and the farmer. If an entire supply of juveniles dies, YDD pays all the costs of the inputs. The farmer loses only the potential income the harvest would have yielded.

Extension Services: Technical Assistance

Pond Preparation. Traditional milkfish ponds can be used to raise tiger prawns after the ponds have been improved. The pond bottom must be excavated because greater water depth is needed; the dikes have to be stabilized and the gates upgraded. Pests and predators are eliminated by drying the pond thoroughly and then applying pesticides. Fertilizing the pond promotes the growth of natural food.

The issue of water depth is especially interesting. Traditional *tambaks* usually consist of a large, shallow middle area that is surrounded by deeper canals. Because milkfish grow well in shallow water, costly excavation is not necessary. The deeper peripheral canals improve the water circulation and allow the milkfish to be easily collected for harvest.

Shrimp prefer deeper water than do milkfish. When tiger prawns are raised in traditional milkfish ponds, they migrate to the deeper canals, which constitute less than 25 percent of the pond area. Water depth can be increased by building higher dikes and pumping water into the pond or by excavating the pond.

Water Management.[14] Pond water contains nutrients and oxygen as well as harmful substances such as chemical pollutants and biological wastes. Thus, constant water management is vital to the successful raising of tiger prawns. The optimal ranges for several water-related operating variables are given below:

- Dissolved Oxygen Level: Minimal acceptable level for shrimp is 2–3 parts per million (ppm). If it is less than 2 ppm, after a period of hyperactivity, the shrimp swim to the surface and die.
- Temperature: Recommended optimal temperature range for food growth and survival rates of shrimp is 25–30° C. At lower temperatures, food growth is reduced; in higher water temperatures, shrimp mortality increases because of poor dissolved oxygen levels.
- Salinity: Tiger prawns grow best in low salinity—about 15 parts per ton (ppt). However, good production can be achieved in traditional ponds under conditions of up to 40 ppt salinity if occasional feedings and regular water exchanges occur.

Major water management tools are pond depth and water exchange. An optimal water depth of 60–100 cm reduces fluctuations in temperatures and dissolved oxygen, increases growth of phytoplankton (natural food) and dilutes biological wastes.

Water exchange replaces oxygen-depleted water with oxygen-rich water, introduces new food (plankton) and carries away biological wastes. Water can be exchanged by tidal action or by using a pump. In tidal water exchange, the pond is partially drained at low tide and then refilled at high tide. By pump, water exchange can be continuous.

Extension Services: Marketing Assistance

Farmers can sell tiger prawns to local middlemen and women or to a cold storage facility. Farmers prefer to sell to local middlemen even for a lower price because they often have some type of social relationship with the buyers, who also serve as the traditional source of credit. Cold storage facilities are located in the cities, usually at a considerable distance from the farmers' *tambaks*. As there is no reliable transport, small *tambak* farmers find it difficult to sell directly to the cold storage facilities.

To solve the marketing problem, YDD established a central marketing network administered by OSU staff. It negotiates agreements with the buyers, organizes deliveries and receives and distributes payments. The OSU staff are more skillful negotiators than are individual pond owners, and the large scale of the OSU operations gives them greater bargaining power.

To avoid displacing the middlemen and women completely and thus cutting the farmers off from their traditional sources of credit, local buyers have been incorporated in the marketing scheme. For example, second-quality prawns that cannot be exported are sold to these buyers for local resale.

First Steps toward Filling the Market Niche:
Understanding the Problems

The YDD/OSU project to promote medium-density shrimp production has two major objectives:

- operating the hatchery as a profitable commercial enterprise, and
- providing assistance to small *tambak* farmers to enable them to switch from traditional milkfish cultivation to the more lucrative cultivation of tiger prawns. These should permit the pond owners to increase their income and thus encourage them to retain ownership of this income-producing resource.

Because the project is still young, it is premature to label it a success or a failure. Since the beginning of OSU in 1988, there have been sixteen harvests, three of which have been profitable. The project encountered two kinds of difficulties in its first two years: social/economic and marketing/technical.

Social and Economic Obstacles

Ownership Structure

Tambak land rights are fluid in Java. Most of the ponds are not owned by one person, but by a family or a number of related farmers. Tenants may also own a percentage of the land they cultivate under a sharecropping system.

A typical arrangement is that of Pak Sumonon, who, with his wife and five children, lives in Bumimulyo. He and his five brothers inherited a one-ha pond from his father. Every year one of them owns the pond, which yields milkfish and salt. In the years when he does not cultivate the pond, Pak Sumonon farms, raising wet rice on one ha of land and dry rice on another 0.5-ha piece of land. When it is his turn to cultivate the pond, a cousin does the rice farming.

Next year, when he will own the pond, Pak Sumonon plans to have it improved. He also expects to sign the YDD/OSU partnership agreement, although this may create problems. The partnership agreement with YDD is for a two-year period, yet he is responsible for the pond only for one year. He has been trying to persuade his brothers to join the partnership program, but they remember the losses incurred by some neighbors. Salt production and milkfish cultivation provide a secure income, although it is less profitable that the potential inherent in intensive tiger prawn production. Pak Sumonon hopes that before he signs the agreement other participants in the YDD program will have enjoyed two or three good shrimp harvests; this success may persuade his brothers to support his decision.

Another aspect of the same problem is the situation of Pak Umbar, a member of the partnership program who has had two successful harvests. After his first successful harvest, his father-in-law claimed the improved pond, which he had given as a present to Pak Umbar fifteen years earlier.

Village and Family Relationships

In addition to the problems presented by the system of group ownership, the project must deal with the strong hierarchical relationships that exist within a family and in a village. The village head is the dominant decision maker. His favoring the OSU program can help to attract new participants. But conflict between the interests of the village head and those of the partnership program can create obstacles for partnership participants.

For example, in Surodadi there are three distinct groups of breeders—the Karya Bundi, Karya Bhakti and Karya Makmur. The groups, which have fifty-eight members among them, hold regular meetings where members exchange information on pond efforts. The village head also is the leader or President of the Karya Bundi group. He favors his own group at the expense of others. Because of an unwritten rule that requires all group meetings to be held in the village hall in the presence of the village head, the other two breeders' groups do not feel free in meetings to openly discuss their activities. Thus, the activities of all the groups are dependent on the ideas and initiatives of the village head.

Families are strictly organized in terms of authority and individual roles. Although strong interrelationships do provide social and economic benefits to a community, they also have negative effects. Such a system can mean that many members earn very little income. There is seldom room for individual actions or for risk taking. If a family member does take risks and increases his income, this extra income must be shared with members of his or her extended family, even though they opposed the initial efforts.

When the project began, the first farmers to enter the partnership program were the wealthier ones. Others, such as the farmers in Surodadi, pursue pond management as a side activity. For example, Pak Nurbadin, the local school teacher, received a 1.8-ha pond as a gift from his father-in-law. Other farmers divide their ponds and their risks in two; they use one part for the project; they use the other to cultivate milkfish.

Investment Costs

The cost to upgrade a pond can be as much as IndRp10,000,000 (US$5,984), depending on its state.[15] The pond must be deepened and equipment such as gates, sluices, and aerators need to be purchased. No one farmer has that much money to invest. Currently, YDD provides the initial credit. But if the partnership program becomes very popular, YDD will have to seek financing from the formal banking systems. Because of the fluid ownership structure, it will indeed be difficult to persuade the banks to make loans to the *tambak* farmers to finance the initial pond improvements. Yet, without investment, intensified shrimp farming is not possible.

In the startup phase, total YDD expenses have exceeded profits, as was expected. At the moment, YDD absorbs the excess costs through grants and loans. As the number of outgrowers increases and the technology is refined, the project is expected to become an independent, commercially viable enterprise. At the time of this study, however, the turnaround had not yet taken place.

Marketing

Because they are the unofficial local bank, local buyers play a crucial role in a village. As it is impossible for small farmers to apply to an official bank for a loan, they depend on these middlemen and women for extra money, for example, in case of an emergency like an illness. Although the interest rates charged by a middleman can be as high as 15 percent per month, farmers prefer dealing with someone they already know.

When the project was designed, it was anticipated that the middlemen and women would lose some of the income they derived from trading in daily catches of shrimp and other fish. To replace the lost income, YDD's Social Monitoring unit has proposed two other income-generating activities—processing of fish and cultivating chilies. Fish can be processed at home; twenty-five pieces of fish sell for IndRp1,500. Although the price of chili is subject to large seasonal fluctuations (from IndRp400/kg to IndRp3,000/kg), chilies can be stored when market prices are low.

The middlemen and women, however, are facing other, unforeseen problems. The demand for quality tiger prawns has been growing and so is the supply. Until recently, because of limited supply, Japan purchased all available tiger prawns—regardless of quality—although in summer of 1988 Japan refused 40 tons of Indonesian tiger prawns because they were inferior.

The best way to ensure a good quality product is to limit the number of players in the marketing channel; ideally, the producers should sell directly to a cold storage facility. This practice would also reduce the cost. But if the local buyers are eliminated, who then will supply credit to the small farmers?

Technical Obstacles

Because raising tiger prawns requires technical skill, it is not surprising that early harvests failed. Experience to date has made clear the need for research and development to solve the following technical problems.

1. Many of the harvest failures can be attributed to too-shallow ponds. The OSU is now aware that ponds must be 60 cm deep and preferably deeper. Most ponds were not this deep and were stocked too densely for the depth; the result was a low survival rate of fry. The lack of communication between those who excavated the ponds and those who stocked

them points out the need for more contact and quality control during the different stages of the shrimp production. Because the density of shrimp in the pond is the basis for calculating additional food supply and necessary oxygen, as well as other measurements, a more accurate way to measure a pond's density should be found.

2. Droughts during the past two years have resulted in a higher than desirable salinity in the ponds, which slowed the growth rate of the tiger prawns. Additional research must be conducted on cost-effective ways to reduce/control salinity (for example, putting in tubewells to pump fresh water) or to locate another type of prawn that would be better adapted to a highly saline environment (for example, the banana prawn).

3. There is need for a feed mix from locally available ingredients that is far less expensive than the presently used imported feed.

4. Finally, research must lead to an increase in the survival rate of the shrimp —in the hatchery, in the nursery and in the *tambaks*—in order that the profitability of raising tiger prawns, both for the small-scale farmers and for YDD, also increases.

Lessons Learned From the YDD/OSU Project

The YDD shrimp cultivation project contains many lessons for improving the venture capital model with which ATI is experimenting. Initially, YDD explored the possibility of investing in a wide array of diverse businesses, ranging from production of *ketjap* (sauce) from wingbeans to production of rattan furniture. The venture capital company's early experiences convinced YDD that it would be better to develop expertise in one particular area of opportunity.

Furthermore, it would be best if this area of opportunity contained both a high-tech and a low-tech component. Profits earned by the high-tech component could be used to serve the poor in a low-tech one. In shrimp cultivation, the high-tech component is the hatchery. Mastering the technology involved in producing fry in the hatchery requires considerable technical expertise, education and training. Because this mastery cannot be accomplished overnight, some protection is afforded against a takeover by a local entrepreneur. The low-tech end—raising the PL21s to maturity—is simple enough to be taught to uneducated farmers.

Thus far, the hatchery has been quite successful. On average, it reports survival rates of 20 percent from hatching to PL21s, which compares favorably with the average 8 percent survival rate reported by other hatcheries in Indonesia.

YDD also has learned the importance of cash flow to its venture capital partners—the small-scale *tambak* farmers. Farmers are willing to make investments, or take risks, only if the returns are visible in the time that they own the pond. Also, small poor *tambak* farmers cannot sustain more than one or two failed harvests. Even if they do not have to pay for the fry that die, they have still lost the earnings from their pond—their only source of cash income.

The need to provide quick turnaround cash and at the same time to reduce risks led to the concept of nursery ponds. In the nursery, PL21s are grown to

PL60s, the juvenile stage, when they have a much better chance of survival in the *tambaks*. Farmers who cultivate juveniles can reap three harvests per year, rather than two. Meanwhile, the juveniles advanced to the farmers command a better price than do PL21s. This is a risk-sharing arrangement in which both parties are winners.

Although YDD has not yet recovered its expenses or its investments in pond improvements, let alone made a profit, the scheme's potential for effectively increasing the productivity of *tambak* farmers has already persuaded the World Bank to provide direct financial assistance to YDD to support this effort.

Notes

1. Private discussion with Carlos Tan, Regional Manager, IFC, August 1988.
2. Wolfgang Hannig and J. A. Setyadi, *A Study on the Potentials of Pond Breeders Development* (Yogyakarta: Yayasan Dian Desa, Mimeograph, 1987), pp. 28–30.
3. In some instances the sharing arrangement may be 60–40.
4. Exchange rate, July 1988, was IndRp1,685 = US$1. *International Financial Statistics* 42(10) (1989).
5. Hannig and Setyadi, pp. 26, 27.
6. *World Bank Report* (Oxford: Oxford University Press, 1988).
7. In 1975 the government started a program called IDA, financed by the World Bank. The main goal was to offer credit facilities to small *tambak* farmers. But only owners of 2-ha ponds or larger were entitled to loans under this program. Loans amounted to IndRp124,000 per hectare at an interest rate of 10.5 percent with a payback period of twelve years. In 1979–1980 a new scheme called RCP was launched, again limited to landowners of two-ha ponds or larger. In addition to the credit facility, technical assistance also is offered. (Wolfgang Hannig, "Innovation and Tenant Survival: Brackishwater Pond Culture in Java," Naga, *The ICLARM Quarterly* April 1988, pp. 5–6.)
8. S. Goldmark and J. Rosengard, *Credit to Indonesian Entrepreneurs: An Assessment of the Badan Kredit Kecamatan Program* (U.S. Agency for International Development, Washington, D.C., 1985). See also R. Kaplinsky, *Economies of Small* (London: IT Publications, 1990).
9. Wolfgang Hannig, *Towards a Blue Revolution, A Study on Socioeconomic Aspects of Brackish Waterpond Cultivation in Java* (Yogyakarta: Yayasan Dian Desa, Mimeograph, 1987), pp. 28–30.
10. Hannig, pp. 67–69.
11. Hannig, p. 70.
12. Hannig, p. 71.
13. Project Plan, Yayasan Dian Desa, p. 20.
14. Project Plan, p. 39.
15. Project Plan, Tables 13 and 15.

8

New Directions: Toward
Mobilizing the Economic
Might of the Informal Sector

How can we best mobilize the economic power of the masses of people who make up the informal sector in order to achieve truly sustainable development? The experiences detailed in the case studies suggest the following guidelines and direction to the authors.

1. Temper Economic Models with Common Sense

First, economists and development practitioners must concur on the economic validity of the income-generating activities of the informal sector. For example, common sense argues that a woman who obtains a small loan to buy fish that she then resells at a higher price has made a profit (earned income) and an economic contribution if her total sales exceed the cost of the loan (capital plus interest) plus other costs (such as transport) of the sales. Yet traditional economists say they cannot attribute negative or positive economic value to the woman's activities because they cannot measure the opportunity cost of her labor or the capital needed.

Another example of the need for a common-sense approach concerns the criticisms leveled at financial programs run by nonfinancial institutions. Critics point out that these programs often do not charge sufficient interest to cover operating expenses, which usually are subsidized by grants. Yet, the authors believe that their positive economic contribution in adding value to locally available production factors more than justifies the marginal subsidies that make these programs possible.

2. Obtain a Better Understanding of the
Risks Faced by the Small-Scale Entrepreneur

To meet the needs of the informal sector, development practitioners must understand the needs, motivations and risks faced by the small-scale entrepreneur. Recent studies indicate that loans might not be the most important need of the informal sector. Even if credit is made available to the informal and rural sectors, how can one reasonably expect a small-scale farmer, a village trader or a landless person to sign a loan—often 100 times the value of his or her annual income—in order to start a business based on an unfamiliar technology? How can one expect people who are landless and have no capital assets to provide collateral to secure a loan? If the potential borrower would continue to work as a laborer, that person would earn some income. Becoming an entrepreneur takes time, but can the potential entrepreneur afford the risks—and provide for a family?

In the coming years, we must strengthen our understanding of these risks and design financial packages that share the risks between the potential entrepreneur and the financial institution. The entrepreneur might need risk capital in the form of equity; short-term loans for working capital; and an emergency fund, basically a type of consumption credit that would (by an overdraft mechanism) finance nonbusiness expenses such as village burials or hospital expenses.

3. Experiment with Various Types of Financial Schemes

Different groups in different countries are experimenting with innovative ways to get capital to the informal sector and have the capital returned—with profits. Established methods of financing such as leasing and franchising are being modified to better serve the informal sector. For example, Islamic banking practices—markup schemes or profit sharing—are reaching target audiences in Iran and Pakistan; the entrepreneur does not have to repay the financing until the enterprise becomes profitable.

Appropriate Technology International (ATI) and other organizations have begun experimenting with adopting the venture capital model to the needs of the informal sector. In the traditional venture capital scheme, the would-be entrepreneur establishes a company in which he or she owns only 10 to 50 percent of the shares; an investment company or venture capital firm holds the remainder. The risk for the venture is shared between the entrepreneur and the venture capital company/investment firm. If the business is successful, the company's assets increase, as do the value of the shares. When the investment firm or venture capital company sells its shares, the profits are its reward for taking the risks of starting a company. If the business fails, the investment firm or venture capital company and the entrepreneur lose their investment.[1]

Although the traditional venture capital scheme is geared primarily to make a profit, the venture capital model is adopted for the informal sector and is geared to reduce the entry barriers for the potential entrepreneur. In the modified approach, the nongovernmental agency (NGO) acts as the venture capital firm; it provides from 70 to 85 percent of the equity, depending on the status of the potential entrepreneurs (the landless, members of a cooperative or a private entrepreneur with a few assets). Because there are so many risks associated with a new technology, the NGO/venture capital company also provides the necessary technical and managerial assistance, similar to the traditional venture capital model.

A new type of financing company—called a Convertible Equity Fund (CEF)—is thought by some to be a solution to the problem of lack of return of capital, encountered in the modified venture capital model. The CEF is being pioneered in the Philippines. In this program, a small enterprise is capitalized through part debt (loan)/part equity (stock) financing. A typical enterprise would be financed with 30 percent equity from the Bank and 20 percent equity from the entrepreneur and incur 50 percent debt. After the enterprise has proved that the technology works—that her/his market expectations are correct—or after a fixed period of say three years, the entrepreneur is required to convert the bank's equity into debt, against the book value of the shares. Thus, the bank is repaid for the greater risk by companies who have done well, by means of a higher book value, or loses because of nonperformance of the company. The financing provides a realistic way to share the risks with the entrepreneur.

CEF financing requires a drastically different approach to banking than is now practiced. The bank must be more closely involved in the enterprise itself. In addition, whereas a bank traditionally would expect repayment of at least 90–95 percent, in this scenario it might have to deal with as many as 50 percent losers. Unlike a traditional loan scheme, however, it will be compensated by a higher return on its capital from the 10 to 20 percent winners. Careful management of its portfolio is mandatory, however, if it is to have these winners.

Additional financial mechanisms used in the formal financial sector such as leasing and franchising are also being tested, in modified forms, in other projects trying to reach informal sector entrepreneurs.

4. Consider the Role Women Play in Development

Until recently, development models did not disaggregate data by gender, despite the fact that women are the major players in the informal sector. Today, any potential development project must, as part of the planning process, consider the program's effect on women. Will women own the new enterprises? Will they be employed in the business? Will women benefit outright—in their own name—or only in the name of a husband or father?

When technology is introduced to mechanize an operation or an activity becomes income earning rather than subsistence, women appear to be forced out of their traditional producer role. This statement is made cautiously as insufficient data are available.[2] But is the overall effect on women beneficial or detrimental—that is, are the women better or worse off? For example, when maize mills were introduced in Cameroon, the women benefited even when they did not own the mills. The time the women saved by not walking long distances to a distant mill, or by having the maize ground by machine rather than grinding it by hand was generally spent in farming their own plots; in most cases, the additional production was sold. When ATI introduced a lease/purchase plan to permit women to own the mills rather than simply be consumers, the women had a chance to earn even more money. Most of the women's groups that were surveyed planned to use at least part of the income derived from the earnings of the maize mill to further increase their income.

This book, by means of specific case studies, has addressed the difficulties encountered in trying to realize the dream of Mahatma Gandhi and others—to create economic structures that facilitate both production by the masses and consumption by the masses. We cannot ignore economic realities. Should Yayasan Dian Desa not have supported improving the productivity of the *tambak* farmers in Indonesia because the tiger prawns are not consumed locally but in Japanese restaurants? The alternative would be to let the industrial conglomerates buy up the land in order to engage in large-scale aquaculture. The *tambak* farmers would receive a fortune for their land, but they would be left without any means of production except their labor.

Viewed from the economic realities of today, development programs that target the poorer section of the population may have to adjust their initial goals of production by the masses, for the masses. In Gandhi's time, industrial production in developing nations was just beginning; now we can see that many of Gandhi's predictions have come true. Urban industrial production has benefited immensely from governmental promotional policies—at the expense of farm and nonfarm activities in rural areas.

Development efforts to improve the conditions of the poor need to focus on increasing the efficiency of production both on the farm as well as in nonfarm activities. Value added in rural areas needs to be become equal or higher than the value added in urban areas. Only this step will reverse the rural-urban migration and fulfill Gandhi's dream of production by and for the masses. In the late 1940s and 1950s the Appropriate Technology (AT) movement was struggling with the problems of production; in the 1980s we have learned that the problems of demand—creating markets—are of equal importance.

But the process of increasing the value added in informal sector operations will not be enough. We need a multifaceted approach. We need to solve problems in the outside environment—the macropolicy environment—to eliminate the distortions in the factors of production, most of which are at present biased against informal and rural small-scale production. We also must work together to create systems that will increase the value of local resources itself. In other words, we need to increase the efficiency of local production by introducing technologies that are as efficient as those used in large-scale, urban-based industries.

To achieve this, national industrialization policies and agricultural development policies will have to be adjusted to give priority to increasing rural productivity. New technologies, such as biotechnology and application of microelectronics, if carefully managed, might play an important role in these policies, as the efficiency of these technologies is not necessarily connected to the scale of the operation. Indeed, new technologies appear to be more scale neutral than technologies developed in the 1970s. Countries such as Taiwan and Costa Rica that have adopted these national industrialization and agricultural development policies have reported substantial increases in rural productivity.[3]

A Holistic Approach to Rural, Small-Scale Income-Generating Activities

How do we get technology into the hands of people and get their products into the marketplace? Simply providing information about technologies and business opportunities rarely accomplishes the objective. Formal credit schemes that target the rural, small-scale enterprise sector have not worked. Training programs for rural entrepreneurs have been ineffective. Trainees from the rural areas stay in the cities and use their skills there.

Three basic goals are evident—and necessary. First, enterprises providing new or improved technologies must actually be established in rural areas. Second, and more difficult, a market, a demand pull, must be created for the products of those enterprises.

As illustrated by the case studies presented in this book, a holistic approach is needed to solve these problems—one that reflects reality rather than a model. It must address the problems of income generation through productive activities in all related fields, from technology to finances to credit, to social, cultural and gender issues.

Third, and most important, we need to understand the primary production factor—the people. What is their motivation to come to work in a small enterprise? What are the risks and advantages? How long will the enterprise be in existence? Will the entrepreneur get paid for the work he or she does? Assumptions that are basic in the industrial advanced countries (IACs) have to be reformulated in terms of the local social and economic situation. For example, in rural areas where there are no hospitals, in times of an accident or serious illness people are completely dependent on the actions of their neighbors, friends or family. As a result, a tight balance of social obligations exists in most villages in the Third World. How does working in a small-scale enterprise complement or conflict with this social structure?

Tomorrow's Goal: A New Ethos

The case studies here describe some of the positive actions that took place in spite of the failures of the central system, but every day newspapers carry the stories of cases in which people decide to achieve their dreams through violent ways. The large number of educated unemployed people in most countries will become a major source of disappointment and disillusionment with the society. Educated to be engineers or administrators, people are forced to lower their expectations. Is it possible to live the lifestyles of the IACs, to sustain the material wealth our generation and the ones before us have achieved in the long term, and to share the wealth with the billions of new people who enter into the world? Our answer, based on common sense and not on economic models, is that it is not. At a world level, governments and individuals are bit by bit mortgaging the future—borrowing more and more not only in financial terms, but also in environmental terms. To enjoy material wealth, we produce goods and wastes that appear to threaten the sustainability of the earth.

But how to change? Many of these changes cannot be made in economic terms. Economic changes are important. More important than these, however, are the illusions that we create about tomorrow, the day after, the next year, our achievements in our life. These are what we have to re-examine—our ethos, our beliefs about life.

This will be the most difficult task of all, to create a new ethos, a new value system that balances the material and social aspects of life. In such a value system, poverty alleviation programs would be combined with income-generating programs. Success would be measured not only by material achievements that cannot be sustained by the available world resources, but also by our ability to share our wealth—in terms of both worldly goods and spiritual resources.

Ideally, this new ethos would be translated into new economic and social objectives. More equal income distribution would be given a higher priority than growth in gross national product (GNP). People living in rural areas would have the same opportunities as those in urban areas to be employed, to earn an adequate income and to take risks to establish their own enterprises.

But a new ethos is still only a dream—and the rural poor in the Third World cannot live on dreams alone. They need concrete actions to help them take the initial steps to help themselves.

Notes

1. Using the equity as collateral, the company obtains loans from banks. In case of bankruptcy, however, the entrepreneur and the venture capital company are liable only for the amount of their investments—a protection the small farmer or individual entrepreneur in a sole proprietorship or partnership unfortunately does not enjoy.

2. M. Carr and R. Sandhu, UNIFEM Occasional Paper No. 6, "Women, Technology and Rural Productivity," United Nations Development Fund for Women, New York, January, 1987.

3. Gustav Ranis and Frances Stewart, "Rural Linkages in the Philippines and Taiwan," in Frances Stewart (ed.), *Macro-Policies for Appropriate Technology in Developing Countries* (Boulder: Westview Press, 1987). See also Eduardo Doryan-Garron, "Macroeconomic Policy, Technological Change and Rural Development: The Costa Rica Case," in Frances Stewart, Henk Thomas, and Ton de Wilde, *The Other Policy* (London: IT Publications, 1990).

✦   Appendix: Appropriate Technology International

APPROPRIATE TECHNOLOGY INTERNATIONAL (ATI) is a private, nonprofit development assistance corporation based in Washington, D.C. It works with organizations and local businesses in Africa, Asia and Latin America to identify, assess, adapt, disseminate and transfer technologies, and to establish commercially viable small-scale enterprises appropriate to the needs and resources of the poor in rural and semi-urban areas of the Third World.

ATI was created in 1976 in response to an initiative by the U.S. Congress to provide "access to tools and machines that are suited to labor-intensive production methods and fit small farms, small businesses, and small incomes." ATI implements its program mainly with funds made available through the U.S. Agency for International Development (USAID) under an agreement with the Bureau of Science and Technology, Division of Employment and Enterprise Development, in the Office of Rural and Institutional Development. ATI also receives funds from other sources and has carried out projects for international organizations and bilateral development agencies.

ATI works through nongovernmental organizations (NGOs) and private institutions to improve the capabilities of small businesses and entrepreneurs. ATI trains local people in the technical aspects of operating equipment, as well as in project planning, financial analysis, management and administration. ATI places a high priority on an enterprise's commercial viability, its ability to create employment and generate income, the project's socioeconomic impact on the rural poor and the potential of the technology for replication elsewhere.

Products and Services

ATI offers the following products and services:

- Establishment of technology-based small and microenterprises in collaboration with local project partners. Between 1984 and 1988, more than

1,280 small and microenterprises were established, creating more than 5,000 jobs. Through backward and forward linkages, 144,000 people increased their incomes. Direct capital investment per workplace averages US$1,500;

- Market assessments for appropriate technologies (end products as well as production processes);
- Design of marketing strategies (including credit programs facilitating the purchase of products) for products of small-scale enterprises;
- Technology assessments for technologies to be utilized in rural areas and market towns;
- Identification of the most efficient technology and provision of technical assistance for processing local resources in rural areas and market towns;
- Commercialization of laboratory-tested technologies intended for use by poor people in rural areas and market towns;
- Identification of macropolicies in the areas of monetary, fiscal, trade and science and technology policies that hinder the application of appropriate technology;
- Replication (transfer) of successful innovations tested in commercially viable, small-scale enterprises from original site to other locations;
- Documentation, publication and communication of ATI's experiences.

Among the products and services provided as part of ATI's long-term strategy are:

- Implementation of programs in collaboration with local project partners that establish clusters of small and microenterprises in sectors of the economy or small geographic regions, introduce microcredit and savings programs and interact with local government authorities to change macro policies to favor appropriate technology;
- Assessment of small-scale industry sectors and subsectors;
- Evaluations of appropriate technology strategies that focus on economic development in small geographic areas or sectors or subsectors of the economy;
- Definition of specific country and regional macro policies that will enhance the impact of technology-based small and microenterprises;
- Design, implementation and/or evaluation of training programs to establish and manage technology-based small and microenterprises.
- Monitoring of ATI Projects.

Once a project is formally approved and funds are committed, ATI staff provides management and technical assistance on a regular basis to implement, monitor and evaluate the project. Based on the specific needs of the project, project officers and evaluation and technical staff visit the project to discuss progress and resolve problems. This multidisciplinary approach to project selection and development is an integral part of ATI's knowledge building and sharing process.

Areas of Expertise

Among ATI's areas of expertise are the following:

- Agricultural Products Processing: Small-scale processing and extracting of edible oils; processing of cereals and staple crops; production of animal feed from agricultural by-products; processing of fruits and vegetables; and the design, modification and manufacture of hand- and machine-powered tools for oil processing and grain milling.
- Equipment and Support for Small Farms: Small-scale applications of biotechnologies, such as rhizobium inoculant for increased soybean yields and protein-enriched cassava for animal feeds, production and marketing of small farm implements, animal-driven water pumps and small-scale rainwater catchment tanks.
- Local Mineral Resources: Small-scale production of cement and related materials; small-scale production and use of lime; production of ceramics, bricks and tiles; improvements in ovens and kilns; and small-scale mining technologies.

ATI promotes market and private sector development by: using nongovernmental organizations as implementing organizations to work with small enterprises; focusing on the commercial viability of technologies and the promotion of small-scale profit-making enterprises; and developing rural small-scale industry projects using innovative financing mechanisms.

✦ Bibliography

Acharya, S., and S. Madhur. "Informal Credit Markets and Monetary Policy." *Economic and Political Weekly*, No. 36 (1984).

Adams, Dale. "Taking a Fresh Look at Informal Finance." Paper prepared for Seminar on Informal Financial Markets in Development. Washington, D.C.: U.S. Agency for International Development, 1989.

Agency for International Development. *The Potential for Financial Innovation in Small and Micro-enterprise Promotion*. Seminar Proceedings. Washington, D.C.: U.S. Agency for International Development, 1988.

Ahmad, Q. K. "Appropriate Technology and Rural Industrial Development in Bangladesh: The Macro Context." In *The Other Policy*, Frances Stewart et al. London: IT Publications, 1990.

Ahmad, Q. K., and F. A. Chowdury. *Rural Industrialization: A Synthesis Based on Studies on Rural Industries Development in Selected Upazilas*. Dhaka: Bangladesh Institute of Development Studies, 1987.

Ahmed, H., and D. Adams, "Transaction Costs in Sudan's Rural Financial Markets." Supplement to *Savings and Development*. Milan: Finafrica, 1987.

Allen, Hugh, et al. "Ceramic Lined Jikos." Project Plan Appropriate Technology International, 1985. Mimeograph.

Anderson, D., and F. Khambata. "Small Enterprises and Development Policy in the Philippines: A Case Study." World Bank Staff Training Paper 468. Washington, D.C.: World Bank, 1981.

Annis, Sheldon. "Can Small-Scale Development be a Large-Scale Policy?" *Development Alternatives: The Challenge for NGOS*. Supplement to *World Development* 15 (1987): 129–34.

Annual Report. Washington, D.C.: Appropriate Technology International, 1987.

Appropriate Technology International. "Regional Wheelchair Production." Washington, D.C.: Appropriate Technology International, 1984. Mimeograph.

Ashe, J. *The PISCES II Experience: Case Studies*. Washington, D.C.: U.S. Agency for International Development, 1985.

Bagachwa, M. S. D. "Technology Choice in Industry: A Study of Grain Milling Techniques in Tanzania." Paper presented at the 1988 International for Conference on the Implications of Technology Choice on Economic Development, Nairobi, Kenya. Washington, D.C.: Appropriate Technology International, August 1988. Mimeograph.

Bautista, R. "Macro-Policies and Technology Choice in the Philippines." In *The Other Policy*. Frances Stewart, et al. London: IT Publications, 1990, pp. 109–38

Berry, Albert. "Price of Capital, Income and Demand for Labor in Developing Countries." *Southern Economic Journal*, 1978.

Bhatt, E. "Women and Small-Scale Enterprise Development in a New Era." Paper submitted to the Ford Foundation Symposium on Expanding Income Earning Opportunities for Women in Poverty, Nairobi, Kenya. New York: Ford Foundation, 1988. Mimeograph.

Biddle, Sinha, M. Farbman and Sillers. "Microenterprise Stock-taking: The Financial Institutions Development, Puskowanjati Women's Cooperative, Maha Bhoga Marga and Yayasan Dian Desa Projects Indonesia." Occasional Paper No. 28. Washington, D.C.: Agency for International U.S. Development, 1989.

Biggs, S. "Irrigation in Bangladesh." Paper prepared for the Conference on the Implications of Technology Choice on Economic Development, Pataya, Thailand. Washington, D.C.: Appropriate Technology International, 1988. Mimeograph.

Biggs, S., and R. Grosvenor-Alsop. "Developing Technologies for the Rural Poor." ITDG Occasional Paper 2. London: IT Publications, 1984.

Bouman, F. J. A. "The ROSCA: Financial Technology of an Informal Savings and Credit Institution in Developing Countries." *Savings and Development* 4(1979):1–24. Milan: Finafrica.

Bouman, F. J. A., and Philippe Bastiaanssen. "Pawnbroking as an Attractive Alternative to Cheap Credit Policy: Cases from India and Sri Lanka." Paper prepared for the Seminar on Informal Financial Markets in Development. Washington, D.C.: U.S. Agency for International Development, 1989.

Bremer, J., et al. *An Analytical Framework for Assistance to the Informal Sector in the Sahel.* Washington, D.C.: U.S. Agency for International Development, 1989.

Carr, Marilyn. "Appropriate Technology and Rural Industrialization." ITDG Occasional Paper 1. London: IT Publications, 1982.

———. "Blacksmith, Baker, Roofing-Sheet Maker. Employment for Rural Women in Developing Countries." London: IT Publications, 1984.

———. *Sustainable Industrial Development.* London: IT Publications, 1988.

Carr, Marilyn, and R. Sandhu. "Women, Technology and Rural Productivity." UNIFEM Occasional Paper No. 6. New York: United National Development Fund for Women, January, 1988.

Chavis, Richard. *Market Analysis of Wheelchairs in Colombia.* Washington, D.C.: Appropriate Technology International, 1988. Mimeograph.

Chen, M. "Development Projects for Women: Oxfam America's Programme in India and Bangladesh." Presented at the conference on The International Women's Decade and Beyond. New York: American Association of University Women, 1986.

Cornia, G. A., R. Jolly and Frances Stewart. *Adjustment with a Human Face.* Oxford: Oxford University Press, 1987.

Cortez, M., A. Berry and A. Ishaq. *Success in Small and Medium Scale Enterprises: The Evidence from Colombia.* New York: Oxford University Press, 1987.

Coughlin, P. "Technology and Industrial Organization: The Kenyan Case." Paper prepared for the Conference on the Implications of Technology Choice on Economic Development, Nairobi, Kenya. Washington, D.C.: Appropriate Technology International, 1988.

Coutts, K. J., H. Guiliani Curry and F. Pellerano. "Stabilisation Programmes and Structural Adjustment Policies in the Dominican Republic." *Labour and Society.* Geneva: International Labour Organization, 1986.

de Gregori, Thomas R. *A Theory of Technology.* Ames: Iowa State University Press, 1985.

de Lancey, Mark W. "Women's Cooperatives in Cameroon: The Cooperative Experiences of the Northwest and Southwest Provinces." *African Studies Review,* March 1987.

de Soto, Hernando. *The Other Path.* New York: HarperCollins, 1989.

Duff, B. "Changes in Small-Farm Paddy Threshing Technology in Thailand and the Philippines." In *Macro-Policies for Appropriate Technology in Developing Countries,* edited by Frances Stewart. Boulder: Westview Press, 1987.

Esguerra, E. F., and R. Meyer. "Collateral Substitutes in Rural Informal Financial Markets: Evidence from an Agricultural Rice Economy." Paper prepared for the Seminar on Informal Financial Markets in Development. Washington, D.C.: U.S. Agency for International Development, 1989.

Farbman, Michael, ed. *The PISCES Studies: Assisting the Smallest Economic Activities of the Urban Poor.* Bureau for Science and Technology Paper No. 4. Washington, D.C.: U.S. Agency for International Development, 1981.

Fricke, T. *High Impact Appropriate Technology Case Studies.* Washington, D.C.: Appropriate Technology International, 1984.

Glaser, T. "Dossier: Small and Medium-Sized Enterprises." *The Courier,* No. 115, Brussels, 1989.

Goldmark, S., and J. Rosengrad. *Credit to Indonesian Entrepreneurs: An Assessment of the Badan Kredit Kecamatan Programme.* Washington, D.C.: U.S. Agency for International Development, 1983.

———. *A Manual to Evaluate Small-Scale Enterprise Programmes.* Washington, D.C.: U.S. Agency for International Development, 1987.

Gomez, A., and V. Saladin. *Programa de Financiamento Microempresas y Grupos Slidarios.* Santo Domingo: Asociación Para el Desarrollo de Microempresas, Inc., 1987.

Grindle, M., et al. *Capacity Building for Scarce Resource Institutions for Small and Micro-Enterprises: A Strategic Overview Paper.* Washington, D.C.: U.S. Agency for International Development, 1987.

Haggblade, Steve, Carl Liedholm and Donald C. Mead. "The Effect of Policy and Policy Reforms on Non-Agricultural Enterprises and Employment in Developing Countries: A Review of Past Experiences." In *The Other Policy,* Frances Stewart et al. London: IT Publications, 1990, pp. 58–98.

Hannig, Wolfgang. "Innovation and Tenant Survival: Brackishwater Pond Culture in Java," Naga, *The ICLARM Quarterly,* April 1988.

———. *Towards a Blue Revolution: A Study on Socioeconomic Aspects of Brackish Waterpond Cultivation in Java.* Yogyakarta: Yayasan Dian Desa, 1988.

Hannig, Wolfgang, and J. A. Setyadi. *A Study on the Potentials of Pond Breeders Development.* Yogyakarta: Yayasan Dian Desa, 1987. Mimeograph.

Harper, Malcolm. *Small Business in the Third World: Guidelines for Practical Assistance.* London: IT Publications, 1984.

Harper, Malcolm, and K. Ramachandran. *Small Business Promotion: Case Studies from Developing Countries.* London: IT Publications, 1984.

Herrick, A. B., et al., eds. *Tanzania: A Country Study.* Washington, D.C.: American University, 1978.

Hospes, Otto. "The Financial Chameleon in Developing Countries: Informal Finance with Case Material From Indonesia." Paper prepared for the Seminar on Informal Financial Markets in Development. Washington, D.C.: U.S. Agency for International Development, 1989.

Hotchkiss, Ralf. *Independence through Mobility: A Guide to the Manufacture of the Appropriate Technology International-Hotchkiss Wheelchair.* Washington, D.C.: Appropriate Technology International, 1984.

Hyman, Eric. "The Design of Micro-Projects and Macro-Policies: Examples from Three of Appropriate Technology International's Projects in Africa." Paper prepared for the Conference on the Implication of Technology Choice and Economic Development, Nairobi, Kenya. Washington, D.C.: Appropriate Technology International, 1988. Mimeograph.

———. "The Economics of Improved Charcoal Stoves in Kenya." *Energy Policy.* London: Butterworth & Co., April 1986.

Hyman, Eric, Arleen Richman and N. Tresp. "Implications of Technology Choice on Economic Development." Report on the Africa Conference: Nairobi, Kenya. Washington, D.C.: Appropriate Technology International, 1989. Mimeograph.

———. "Implications of Technology Choice on Economic Development." Report on the Asia Conference: Pataya, Thailand. Washington, D.C.: Appropriate Technology International, 1989. Mimeograph.

International Fund for Agricultural Development. *Credit to the Poorest: The Grameen Bank, Bangladesh and the Small Farmers' Development Program.* Rome: International Fund for Agricultural Development, 1987.

International Labor Organization. *Technological Change, Basic Needs and the Conditions of Rural Women.* Report of the Joint ILO/Government of Northern Africa Regional Project. Geneva: ILO World Employment Program, 1984.

Izumida, Yoichi. "The Kou in Japan: A Precursor of Modern Finance." Paper prepared for the Seminar on Informal Financial Markets in Development. Washington, D.C.: Appropriate Technology International, 1989.

Jackelen, H., R. G. Blayney and J. MacGill. "Evaluation of PRODEM Program in Bolivia." Washington, D.C.: U.S. Agency for International Development, 1987.

———. "Appropriate Technology in Sugar Manufacturing." In *Macro-Policies for Appropriate Technology in Developing Countries,* Frances Stewart. Boulder: Westview Press, 1987.

Kaplinsky, R. *Economies of Small: Appropriate Technology in a Changing World.* London: IT Publications, 1989.

———. "Sugar Processing in India and Kenya." Paper presented at the Nairobi Conference on Macro Policies and Impact on Technology Choice and Small Scale Development. Washington, D.C.: Appropriate Technology International, 1988. Mimeograph.

J. Keddie, R. Nanjundan and R. Tezler. *Development of Rural Small Industrial Enterprise.* Vienna: United Nations Industrial Development Organization, 1988.

Kilby, P., and Carl Liedholm. *The Role of Non-Farm Activities in the Rural Economy.* New Delhi: World Congress of International Economics Association, 1986.

Korten, David C. "Third Generation NGO Strategies: A Key to People-Centered Development." *Development Alternatives: The Challenge for NGOS.* Supplement to *World Development* 15 (1987): 145–59.

Lamberte, Mario B. "Informal Finance and the Manufacturing Sector: The Case of the Footwear Industry in the Philippines." Paper prepared for the Seminar on Informal Financial Markets in

Development. Washington, D.C.: U.S. Agency for International Development, 1989.

Lantam, A. N. "Types of Informal Groups in the North West Province and How They Are Being Used as Intermediaries for Rural Credit." Talk given Oct. 30, 1986.

Levitsky, J. *Review of World Bank Lending to Small Enterprises*. Washington, D.C.: World Bank, 1987.

———. *Microenterprises in Developing Countries*. London: IT Publications, 1989.

Levitsky, J., and R. Prasad. "Credit Guarantee Schemes for Small and Medium Enterprises." Washington, D.C.: World Bank, 1987.

Liedholm, Carl. "Small-Scale Enterprise Dynamics and the Evolving Role of Informal Finance." Paper prepared for the Seminar on Informal Financial Markets in Development. Washington, D.C.: U.S. Agency for International Development, 1989.

Liedholm, Carl, and E. Chuta. "The Economies of Rural and Urban Small-Scale Industries in Sierra Leone." African Rural Economy Paper No. 14. East Lansing: Michigan State University, 1977.

Liedholm, Carl, and Donald C. Mead. "Small-Scale Enterprises in Developing Countries: Empirical Evidence and Policy Implications." MSU International Development Working Paper No. 9. East Lansing: Michigan State University, 1987.

Madeley, John. "Cameroon Reaps Rewards." *Development Forum*. May 1987.

Mann, Charles K., Merilee Grindle and Parker Shipton. *Seeking Solutions: Framework and Cases for Small Enterprise Development Programs*. West Hartford: Kumarian Press, 1989.

Marshall, K. *Package Deals: A Study of Technology Development and Transfer.* London: IT Publications, 1983.

McKee, Katherine. "Micro Level Strategies for Supporting Livelihood. Employment and Income Generating for Poor Women in the Third World: The Challenge of Significance." Paper submitted to the Ford Foundation Symposium on Expanding Income Earning Opportunities for Women in Poverty: A Crossregional Dialogue, Nairobi, Kenya, 1988.

Meadows, Donella, et al. *The Limits to Growth: A Report for the Club of Rome to Project on the Predicament of Mankind.* New York: Universe Books, 1972.

Medellin, Rodrigo. "Informal Credit: To the Campesino Word of Honor in Mexico." Paper prepared for the Seminar on Informal Financial Markets in Development. Washington, D.C.: U.S. Agency for International Development, 1989.

Namuye, Sylvester A. *Survey on Dissemination and Impact of Ceramic Jikos in Kenya*. Nairobi: Energy and Environment Organizations, 1988.

Ncube, P. D. "The International Monetary Fund and the Zambian Economy." In Havenik, K. J. (ed.), *The IMF and the World Bank in Africa*. Uppsala: Scandinavian Institute of African Studies, 1987.

Ndlela, Daniel B. "Macro-policies for Appropriate Technology in Zimbawean Industry." In *The Other Policy*, Frances Stewart, et al. London: IT Publications, 1990, pp. 167–85.

Nelson, N., et al. "Foreign Area Studies for 1974." *Area Handbook for the United Republic of Cameroon.*

O'Kelly, Elizabeth. *Rural Women: Their Integration in Development Programs and How Simple Intermediate Technologies Can Help Them.* London: IT Publications, 1987.

Ohio State University, U.S. Agency for International Development and the World Bank. Seminar on Information Financial Markets in Development. Washington, D.C., October 18–19, 1989.

Onchan, Tongroj. "Informal Rural Credit in Thailand: An Overview." Paper prepared for the Seminar on Informal Financial Markets in Development. Washington, D.C.: U.S. Agency for International Development, 1989.

Otero, Maria. *Gender Issues in Small Scale Enterprise.* The Gender Manual Series. Washington D.C.: U.S. Agency for International Development, 1987.

———. *A Question of Impact.* Tegucigalpa, Honduras: PACT, 1987.

Otero, Maria, and J. Downing. "Meeting Women's Financial Needs: Lessons for Formal Financial Institutions." Paper prepared for the Seminar on Informal Financial Markets in Development Washington, D.C.: U.S. Agency for International Development, 1989.

Painter, Flora M. *Informal Sector and Economic Institutional Reform* (Final Draft), including annotated bibliography of documents on the informal sector. Washington, D.C.: U.S. Agency for International Development, 1989.

Pasecki, R. "Appropriate Technology in Sub-Saharan Africa." Paper prepared for the Conference on the Implications of Technology Choice on Economic Development, Nairobi. Washington, D.C.: Appropriate Technology International, 1988.

Patel, V. G. *Innovations in Banking: the Gujarat Experiments.* World Bank Domestic Finance

Studies, No. 51. Washington, D.C., 1978.

Patten, R. H., and R. Snodgrass. "Monitoring and Evaluating KUPEDES." Development Discussion Paper No. 249. Cambridge: Harvard Institute of International Development, 1987.

Perry, Edward. "Adapted Maize Mill Production in Cameroon." *Appropriate Technology International Bulletin* 12, November 1987.

———. "A Key to Success: Institutional Infrastructure." *Macro Policies and Appropriate Technologies Stimulate Small Enterprise Development.* Appropriate Technology International Annual Report, 1987.

———. "ATI Project Plan, Anguh Maize Mill." Washington, D.C.: Appropriate Technology International, 1985. Mimeograph.

Poyo, J., D. Hoelscher and M. Malhotra. "Microenterprise Stock Taking: The Dominican Republic." Occasional Paper No. 24. Washington, D.C.: U.S. Agency for International Development, 1989.

Prabowo, Dibyo. "The Role of Informal Financial Intermediation in the Mobilization of Household Savings and Allocations in Indonesia." Paper prepared for the Seminar on Informal Financial Markets in Development. Washington, D.C.: U.S. Agency for International Development, 1989.

Project Plan. *LAC Regional Wheelchair Production.* Washington, D.C.: Appropriate Technology International, 1984.

Ranis, Gustav. "Rural Linkages and Choice of Technology." In *The Other Policy,* Frances Stewart et al. London: IT Publications, 1990, pp. 43–57.

Ranis, Gustav, and Frances Stewart. "Rural Linkages in the Philippines and Taiwan." Paper prepared for the Conference on the Implications of Technology Choice on Economic Development, Pataya, Thailand. Washington, D.C.: Appropriate Technology International, 1988. Mimeograph.

Rojas, Jose Luis. "Commercial-Economic Evaluation: Swine Feed Delivery System for Small Farmers." *Evaluation Report.* Washington D.C.: Appropriate Technology International, 1987. Mimeograph.

Sanderatne, Nimal. "Informal Lenders in Sri Lanka: Linking Formal and Informal Markets." Paper prepared for a Seminar on Informal Financial Markets in Development. Washington, D.C.: U.S. Agency for International Development, 1989.

Santikarn, M. "Macro-Policies for Appropriate Technology: Case Studies in Thailand." Paper prepared for Conference on the Implications of Technology Choice on Economic Development, Pataya, Thailand. Washington, D.C.: Appropriate Technology International, 1988. Mimeograph.

Secretaria de Estado Agricultura, Dirección General de Ganaderia. *Situación y Perspectivas de la Produción Porcina en la República Dominicana.* Santo Domingo: Secretaria de Estado Agricultura, 1985.

———. *Censo Porcino Julio 1984 y Muestro Porcino Junio 1985.* Santo Domingo: Secretaria de Estado Agricultura, 1985.

Seibel, H. D. "Upgrading Informal Financial Institutions: NGOs and Self-Help Groups Establish Their Own Banks in Indonesia." Paper prepared for the Seminar on Informal Financial Markets in Development. Washington, D.C.: U.S. Agency for International Development, 1989.

Selbstad, Jennifer. *Struggle and Development Among Self-Employed Women: A Report on the Self-Employed Women's Association in Ahmedabad, India.* Washington, D.C.: U.S. Agency for International Development, 1982.

Sinha, S. "Planning for Rural Industrialization." ITDG Occasional Paper No. 8. London: IT Publications, 1983.

Smillie, Ian. *No Condition Permanent: Pump Priming Ghana's Industrial Revolution.* London: IT Publications, 1986.

Smith, John Guy, et al. *Wheelchairs for the Third World.* Washington, D.C.: Appropriate Technology International, 1984.

Solem, Richard Ray. *A New Look at Small Farmer Credit.* Washington, D.C.: U.S. Agency for International Development, 1990.

Statistical Abstract of the United States. Washington, D.C.: Government Printing Office, 1988.

Stewart, Frances. *Macro-Policies for Appropriate Technology in Developing Countries.* Boulder: Westview Press, 1987.

Stewart, Frances, Henk Thomas and Ton de Wilde, eds. *The Other Policy: The Influence of Policies on Technology Choice and Small Enterprise Development.* London: IT Publications, 1990.

Story, C. *The Latin American Times,* Vol. 7, No. 8, London, 1986.

Streeten, Paul. "Development Dichotomies." *World Development* 10 (1983).

Strutz, Christian. "Technical Assessment: Swine Feed Delivery System for Small Farmers." *Evaluation Report*. Washington, D.C.: Appropriate Technology International, 1987. Mimeograph.

Swartzendruber, J. F. "Changing Policy in Zimbabwe: Sunflower Seed Press." In *Appropriate Technology International 1987 Annual Report*. Washington, D.C.: Appropriate Technology International, 1988.

Tomecko, Ndugu James. "Alternative Strategies for Developing Pottery in Tanzania." SIDO Seminar Proceedings. Arusha, April 1977.

Toukam, Jean Bosco. "Maize Milling in North West Province of Cameroon: A Survey of Existing Practices." In Edward Perry, "ATI Project Plan, Anguh Maize Mill." Washington, D.C.: Appropriate Technology International, 1985. Mimeograph.

United Nations Publications. "The Effectiveness of Industrial Estates in Developing Countries." New York: United Nations, 1988.

US Agency for International Development. "The Potential for Financial Innovation in Small and Micro-enterprise Promotion." Proceedings from a seminar held January 28, 1988, Washington D.C.

Wangwe, S. M., and M. S. D. Bagachwa. "Impact of Economic Policies on Technological Choice and Development in Tanzanian Industry." Paper prepared for the Conference on the Implications of Technology Choice on Economic Development, Nairobi, August 1988.

World Bank. *World Development Report 1988*. Oxford: Oxford University Press, 1988.

World Bank. *Project Plan for the Implementation of the Hatchery and Outgrowers Service Unit*. Yogyakarta: Yayasan Dian Desa, 1987.

Index